YOU ARE
THE PRODUCT

Powerful Self-Marketing
For Practicing Professionals

By
Lester W. Anderson
with
Shelley A. Lee

Financial Marketing Group, Inc.

YOU ARE
THE PRODUCT
Powerful Self-Marketing
For Practicing Professionals

Lester W. Anderson
with
Shelley A. Lee

Copyright © 1993 Lester W. Anderson and Shelley A. Lee

Published by
Financial Marketing Group, Inc.
P.O. Box 9
Avondale Estates, GA 30002

Library of Congress Catalog Card Number: 92-75975

ISBN 0-9634809-4-4
$29.95 Hardcover

YOU ARE
THE PRODUCT
Powerful Self-Marketing
For Practicing Professionals

By
Lester W. Anderson
with
Shelley A. Lee

The authors are available for speaking or consulting engagements. They may be contacted at Financial Marketing Group, Inc., P.O. Box 9, Avondale Estates, GA 30002

This book is dedicated to the hundreds — even thousands — of financial service professionals who have influenced us over the years. We are grateful for the ideas and knowledge we have gained from them and hope that this book inspires them as they have us. We are also indebted to our families, friends, and business colleagues for their encouragement and support during the time we spent working on this project.

L.W.A
S.A.L.
January, 1993

Table of Contents

INTRODUCTION

I bargained with Life for a penny,
and Life would pay no more,
However I begged at evening
When I counted my scanty store;

For Life is just employer,
He gives you what you ask,
But once you have set the wages,
Why, you must bear the task.

I worked for a menial's hire,
Only to learn, dismayed,
That any wage I had asked of Life,
Life would have paid.

Jessie B. Rittenhouse, "The Door of Dreams"

INTRODUCTION

In November, 1989, the cover story of Money magazine was titled "Avoid the Jokers." It offered criteria to help consumers find an honest stockbroker, insurance agent, financial planner, or other financial pro. Joker or broker. Joker or planner. Joker or agent. Joker or accountant. The story implied that one has to look very, very hard to find an honest professional. That is simply not true, and many of us in the financial services profession were rightfully miffed.

I recall this incident for you because, despite the article's negative slant, it still serves as a positive example of the primary premise of this book — you *are* the product. Consumers really want to "buy" people, not just products and services from people.

There are thousands of others out there just like you who are selling professional services and products, but who are failing to sell themselves. In an era of generic, "me too" products that your clients and prospects can get from institutions as diverse as their corner bank or a long-distance discount broker, what most of them are not getting is what they really want — YOU.

You know from the title of this book and the opening above that we are going to talk about marketing yourself. So you may be asking, "Okay, Lester W. Anderson, exactly who are you and why are you qualified to tell me how to market myself?"

The Anderson File

You've heard of a college dropout, right? Well I'm a college throwout. There is a big difference between being dropped and thrown — it has to do with the way you land.

I went away to college in the Fall of 1962, and I quickly got good at the "social" side of college, partaking of all the fun things a warm-blooded American college boy is supposed to. In fact, I got good at everything except studying. In the spring of my first year the Dean decided that my athletic and social prowess did not outweigh my academic shortcomings as I had secured a GPA with the decimal point all the way to the left.

The Dean decided I needed to be somewhere, but not there — so he tossed me out. When something like that happens to you, you want to do something dramatic. You want to do something that says to that person who made that judgment: you made an error; you are wrong about me. I decided to do something dramatic — I joined the Marine Corps. That'd show 'em.

I came back to the U.S. in 1967 after a four-year hitch in the Marines and a tour in Southeast Asia and got involved in an arranged marriage. My mother and this young lady's mother got together while I was in Vietnam and decided that we should get married. As you know from reading my bio, I'm a good old Southern boy and any good old Southern boy does what his Mama tells him. I married the girl.

This arranged marriage has had a profound influence on my life. My wife and I recently celebrated our 25th anniversary and the good Lord willing we'll celebrate another 25. Marriage taught me some early lessons in "real life" — like the fact that there has to be an income to sustain it — and so I ventured into sales and marketing, which taught me even more lessons in real life. When I was in high school and college, there was always food in the refrigerator and clothes to wear. Those clothes were even *trained*. I could throw them on the floor and they would get themselves washed, dried, folded, and back in the closet and drawers. (I have not been able to teach them to do that since then.) If I needed the keys to the car and a little pocket money, I could get them both. It was a pretty good life, when you think about it.

When I went into the Marine Corps, it was pretty much the same thing. They gave me money every month and if I managed to blow it all in town on wine, women, and song I still had a place to sleep, food to eat, and those stylish clothes the Corps issues. When I got out of the Corps and got married I found, to my dismay, that the world had changed.

I went back to school on my $125 a month from the GI bill and $13 a month in combat disability pay and . . . it was just not quite enough. We were usually a buck or two short. My wife went to work and she earned maybe $100 a week, but we need-ed a little more. So I took a part-time job as a door-to-door commission salesman, going out in the evenings and knocking on the doors of the houses of perfect strangers, not knowing whether or not they'd slam the door in my face. After all, they had never heard of me, the company I worked for, or the product I was selling. My task was to say something interesting enough to get inside the home and in front of the homeowners, present my wares, sell some, collect the money, and exit — never to be seen or heard from again.

The company I went to work for had told me, "Les, we're going to pay you 20 cents on every dollar you sell." Tantalized by the imminent fort-une I saw in my future I said, "How much can I make, guys?" You know what they told me: "As much as you want. Just bust your sides."

So I went out there week after week and did just that, and I got pretty good at it. I made $140 or $150 a week part-time, *while* I was also in school full-time, an amount that was more than most full-time people were making in 1967.

After about 10 weeks of getting better and better, my employers said, "Les, we would like you to make more." When you are on commission and "they" tell you they want you to make more, what is the natural assumption about what they want you to do? Sell more! So I said, "Wait a minute, guys. I'm a married man. I have a family and I'm in school full-time. I'm only doing this part-time." They said, "Oh yes, we know. We're not interested in you selling more. Just keep up your own level of sales. But we would like you now to begin *marketing*."

I was confused. I said, "Marketing, selling — it's all the same thing. You know, interacting with the customer." "No, no, no," they said. "Marketing and selling are two distinctly different operations."

If you take few other things away from reading this book, take this one thought: marketing is *declarative*. It is statement-driven — e.g. "This coffee is *great*." Selling, on the other hand, is an *interrogative* process which requires questions and the participation of another party — e.g. "Would you like a cup of this great coffee?" Marketing is much more a one-way process. I was about to learn that.

My employers said to me, "We would like you to hire a couple of other people and teach them what you're doing. We'll pay you a little commission on everything they do, too." Naturally, I asked, "Well, how many can I have?" They said, "Just as many as you want."

Two years later as a rising senior at East Carolina University I had 850 part-time and full-time salespeople working for me. That year, I earned $109,000 while carrying a full-time load. Remember, *this was 1969.* That was about the same amount of money as the entire English department got paid. (If nothing else, it taught me that I didn't want to teach in academia.) I stayed with that company four more years, traveling the country, hiring, developing, and training sales people and teaching salespeople how to sell and managers how to manage.

I've seen a lot of changes in "marketing" in my 25 professional years and although in *some* respects marketing is marketing through the years, in other respects marketing (like most other disciplines, arts, or sciences) undergoes tremendous change as the entity of the marketplace — people — changes. It's certainly changed since 1967, and is continuing to evolve.

You can see evidence that marketing is a declarative process all around you. There is even a mini-trend of new ads today that use bold, almost arrogant, tag lines as part of their marketing message. "Subaru. What to drive." .... "Miller Lite. It's It And That's That." .... "A-1. It's how steak is *done.*" .... "Beef. It's what's for dinner." ...."BMW. The Ultimate Driving Machine" ... Contrast these with the decades-old "Wouldn't you really rather have a Buick?" (*"Well, no thanks, I'll have one of those Mustangs . . ."*)

We're going to discuss these and other principles of marketing at more length later and you'll see that most of them are predicated on changes in consumer buying habits, demographic shifts, consumer expectations, and the ways in which adult consumers "process" information.

In 1974 I returned to school — enrolled in the M.B.A. program at Wake Forest University. I also did some advanced studies in adult education to figure out how and why you and I, as adults, learn — how and why we absorb and apply information that causes us to take action.

We really do learn differently from young people. There are two basic reasons for that. The first is that the "chemistry" in our bodies changes as we get older, and not just in comparison to the hormonal sap of puberty. The chemistry that surrounds a person's brain literally causes it to function differently at different ages. This process never stops as we age.

The second reason is that, as adults, we have certain "blocks" to learning, barriers that impede the process of learning new things. As adult learners, we are contaminated. We have brains on which someone has written: "You can't do this. That won't work. This is dumb." And, more times than not, we believe it! We develop what psychologists call "premature dismissal."

As young persons, we learn *conceptually*. We accept concepts and ideas in good faith and we apply them — our brains are clean sheets that will accept these concepts without resistance.

Almost all the learning that takes place for us as adults is done *experientially*, which means that the new ideas that we learn and the new skills we develop must be tied in some way to an experience — one that already exists within us, that we have had a chance to put into practice, and on which we have received feedback.

This is a very important point to remember when dealing with your clients and prospects. *They learn only when you tie new ideas to some knowledge that is already present.* In presentations, as you introduce new ideas and new concepts, make sure you link them in some way to whatever already exists in the client's head. Author G. K. Chesterton (1874-1936) once said, "The chief object of education is not to learn things but to *unlearn* things." Your prospects and clients will test you.

After my own studies in adult learning, I became a consultant traveling the country and working for various companies, ultimately focusing more specifically and narrowly on the financial services market. Today, I am an employee of a major mutual fund distributor, a company that came to me as a client in 1986 and which later hired me to help their sales force become better public speakers.

Over the last six years I've been in front of, next to, around, and beside more than 20,000 stockbrokers, planners, insurance agents, accountants, and legal and medical professionals all over the U.S, Canada, Australia, and New Zealand, learning about and examining how they do business. This book is dedicated to, and is in large part a result of, the people with whom I have worked, the practices they have, and the ideas I have helped them with that are doing one thing: driving revenue to higher levels.

You are in the commission/fee/revenue producing business; if you don't believe it try *not* producing revenue or commissions for about a month and see what happens. You do all the wonderful, honest, hardworking, ethical, service-oriented things you do for your clients because it's the right thing, but you are in the business of generating income — for yourself and your company. What I hope you will learn from this book is how to move from a product or service-focused practice to a market-focused practice. These new techniques and marketing strategies will result in higher fees and commissions — *more personal revenue.*

Now for some good news about higher fees and commissions: many of you are already realizing them. A recent report by the Securities Industry Association said that average annual gross production for registered representatives jumped 23 percent in 1991. The year's rise in average broker earnings — to $98,401 — is the third consecutive yearly increase. Median rep production was $173,467. The SIA's report noted that, because of favorable stock market conditions, broker production was expected to rise another 20 percent in 1992.

It's safe to assume that a lot of investment professionals out there made more money last year on the market's coattails — still being "transaction oriented." But I also believe that the really smart ones are doing well because they've shifted their focus to *marketing* — not just making trades in a bull market. (Don't forget: the bull market *will*, some day, some time, come to an end.)

If you shift your focus to *marketing* you will be able to better weather the peaks and valleys, the boom-and-bust cycles, that are a natural force in business. There will always be booms and people who build their businesses around them, an often fatal short-term flaw. Where are all the financial practitioners from the early and mid-'80s who "only did tax shelters"? They're bust — in a new career in a different industry or starting over with new clients or, quite possibly, in jail! Where are all those who, in the mid-'80s, "only did government enhanced/hedged bond funds" that were paying 12 to 14 percent? After the bonds were called, the field was culled.

Changing your focus to marketing, not selling, is also about learning the skills you need to get greater exposure and higher visibility in your marketplace. Max Carey, president of Corporate Resource Development, a consulting firm in Atlanta, Ga., says, "Competition demands that we improve our skills or be passed by. As the market changes and evolves, the strategies required to change and be successful must also change."

If you adopt new marketing strategies you will improve personal sales by transitioning your marketing to where the large profits wait. To do that, you must gain knowledge that supports and builds your business. You must be willing to embrace change — real, substantive change — and evolution. With these things will come personal growth.

The failure to adapt what you do and how you do it as demands in the marketplace shift either radically or imperceptibly *will lead to your extinction.* Are your clients the same today as they were five years ago? Is their knowledge level higher? Do they think and act differently today than they did five years ago? 10 years ago?

Skip Massengill, a six figure-plus broker with Butcher & Singer in Philadelphia, Pa., and one of the Top 10 Brokers in the U.S. as selected by Registered Representative magazine, notes that, while some things *never* change — "clients always want the *best* investment at the *cheapest* price with the *least* amount of risk" — many things have changed for those of us who provide professional services, especially in the financial services industry.

"Consumers are being absolutely bombarded with information on products and services," says Skip. "It's terribly confusing to them. A lot of the time, they just know that their neighbor says 'I'm doing this' and so that makes it okay. We have to change what we're doing in order to get clients away from this short-term 'fix-it' approach. That depends greatly on how people see you as a professional."

Change is unsettling; we all know that. It is also invigorating, stimulating, enriching — and, ultimately, profitable. You should not fear failure. You should fear the failure to make change.

Summary — Introduction:

• *Selling is not marketing, and vice versa. Marketing is developing methods that multiply your impact in the marketplace.*
• *Markets — the people who buy products and services— are in a constant state of change.*
• *The end of the "product solution" era is at hand. The advantage of one product over another—if there is any—is no longer what consumers are seeking.*
• *Children learn conceptutally. Adults learn experientially. Your prospects and clients will learn from you only when you tie a new idea to some knowledge that already exists.*

1

DIVIDE AND CONQUER

"If I shoot at the sun I may hit a star."

P. T. Barnum

1

Let's play a game.

Pretend that you have developed this great new product—a *terrific* product. You have a choice: you can market it yourself, building your own company and "going for it," or you can have it licensed and someone else can sell it for you. Your entrepreneurial spirit (the same one that leads you to take the risks inherent in working on a commission or fee basis) tells you to "go for it!"

Up and away you go with your new company and your new product. Your expectations of sales the day you hang out your sign is that they will go right up through the roof. *This is a great new product. It's terrific.* After all, you invented it. Your friends, your spouse, your mother, your dog — they all think it's terrific, too.

Day one comes along, the day you roll out the product and introduce it to the marketplace, and . . . not much happens. You have this problem: you must cross a certain "barrier" in terms of sales performance. That barrier is called "costs" or "break-even" and you have to get across this barrier to begin making money. After all, you are not taking this risk to lose money.

Psychologists tell us that our behavior is driven by hopes, fears, desires, and wishes. Your hope, as founder of a young company, is that consumers will recognize the value and desirability of your product and, once they do that, the products will just fly off the shelves. So you begin to do the things that generate recognition for your product.

Sure enough, as time passes, "they" do recognize how wonderful your product is, sales begin to add up, and you get over the break-even line. You allow yourself to hope for a little more: to move beyond just market recognition into true market acceptance. To have that acceptance means people will buy your products over and over and over again.

They do! Sales are coming along nicely. In a few years you take your company public; in a few more years, chafing at questions from those pesky stockholders, you do a private leveraged buy-out. Oops, need more capital. You go public again. Public, private, public, private. About three jerks of the handle and you're filthy rich and having tea and crumpets at the Waldorf Astoria, enjoying your new success. Now you face another barrier — the one veteran marketers refer to as a product going "shelf stale", or flat in the market. "Oh yeah, I think I have one of those things in my closet." Sales flatten.

Guess who shows up about this time? Old man competition, who says, "Gosh, this is a great product and I think it works well." *I think I can make a better product and get into this marketplace and make a lot of money and have tea and crumpets at the Waldorf Astoria, too.*

When old man competition shows up, your market share starts to contract, along with your margins. That's because that margin, the difference between the selling price and the manufacturing and distribution cost, is being squeezed. After all, old man competition has relied on *you* to develop the marketplace. Soon, sales and margins become so contracted that the risk of continuing to do business far exceeds any potential reward. When that happens, when you can no longer "win," you throw in the towel.

The premier marketing companies of the world have seen this happen over and over again. They developed a product; sales took off; sales flattened; sales finally fell precipitiously. In a graphic sense, this phenomenon forms a bell curve.

In the "old days" of product marketing, there was someone from accounting, sales, marketing, distribution, and manufacturing — a committee to manage what happened with the product. Ushering in a new era in product marketing, some of these premier marketing companies introduced a new idea, a new concept of marketing a product. They annointed a single person to control all of the activities for that product — it was the birth of the Brand Manager. That single person, with all responsibility for the product, had as one of his or her key tasks to recognize this window in time, this point at which sales are about to go flat, and to articulate and implement some strategic change for the product.

Think about what happens to a well-known consumer product like Tide or Crest about every two or three years. It becomes "new and improved." The manufacturer does something — *something* to juice up the product. They put a brightener in it; a freshener in it; a spout on it; they put it in a pump. But they do something to meet changes in the market. When this change occurs you get a new bell curve of sales — the strategic change curve.

Hitting The Wall

"What does that have to do with me?", you ask. "I'm a professional who sells services." Are you telling me that you haven't yet reached, or don't anticipate reaching any time in the future, a place where revenues go flat? Actually, first they go sort of sideways. When that happens to you or your buddy in the next office we say you've plateaued. And the real true part of that is the "teaued" (toad) part — there's no hop left. If someone tells you you've plateaued, they are saying you don't have anything else to give; you are done for.

I submit to you that there is no such thing as a

plateau. It's a state of mind.   There is, however, a wall there, a wall holding you back, a wall that is preventing you from moving forward.   There is a sure and solid barricade as fixed as any brick wall you can run up against and it is holding you back. This wall is made up of certain solid blocks or segments *that are conquerable.*

The first thing you have to do is identify what's holding you back. First, a question in this little exercise. You all know brokers, planners, agents, or consultants who do a million, million and a half, two million a year in gross commissions and fees. How do they do it and you don't? Are they smarter than you? No! Do they work harder than you? No! They probably don't work *as* hard. Were they preordained to produce $2,000,000 while you gen-erate $75,000? No, that didn't happen either. Why do they drive so much business and you don't?

They figured out what was in the wall and how to break through it. What is it that's holding you back? Why can't you move ahead? Why do you seem to be trapped in this lower productivity level?

You Didn't Tell Me It Was Going To Be Like This

To illustrate what's in the wall and how to break through it, let's pretend you are a "typical" stock-broker.

As a youthful practicing professional, what did you do to drive business? You remember . . . . you went to school and got trained, got licensed or accredited, and you were cut loose on the public. The public hasn't been the same since.

As a young "financial consultant" or "account executive," you began under the care and feeding of a manager. How did your manager tell you to market? What is the first tool he or she gave you? Well, what is the average stockbroker still doing? Making 10,000 telemarketing calls a year. Your manager handed you a phone and a phone book and said, "Here, bust your sides."

When you walk into a brokerage or planning office you can always spot the rookies — they are sitting in a dark corner beating up on a telephone. Calling, calling, calling. They are dropping these tickets, like so many pieces of confetti, into a commission bucket, and they barely cover the bottom. The rookies are doing $40 to $50 a day, gross. They are hammering them out one at a time on the phone.

Everybody in brokerage management can tell you what happens about the 90th day of a rookie's career.

He walks into the manager's office. He's listing about 10 degrees to starboard. He is bent over a little, like somebody has beat him with a rubber hose. He looks at the manager and says, "Oh . . . . you didn't tell me it was going to be like this."

Think what is happening to this poor rookie.

He has been told, over and over again, "I don't want any." "How did you get my name?" "Take me off your list." "I have somebody who does that for me." "Go to hell." Dial tone . . . You can tell when somebody on the other end of the rookie's instrument of torture says, "Mail me some information." A little ray of sunshine sneaks into that dark corner, and you can see that rookie headed to the literature closet, smiling to himself, saying, "I get to mail something out today!" He is so happy he can't stand it. Somebody, *somebody* did not beat him up on the phone.

Most experienced brokers would love to have the postage back on all that fabulous literature they mailed out. In some cases they could retire on the postage alone.

What is the next can't-miss "campaign" the rookie uses to go to market? Cold calls first, then mass mailers. Letters, cards, newsletters, brochures, flyers, and a whole host of other printed matter sent out over and over and over. Some consultants (usually those who make their living in direct-mail) will say, "Buy a computer; send out 5,000 pieces; send them five or six times. Wear 'em down." (They will even be glad to sell you a system for ten or twenty thousand dollars.)

Who is the greatest source of mass mailers? Product sponsors or consultants who want to sell you these mailers, charge you a fee, or encourage you to sell their products.

The wholesaler or consultant walks in, sees

the rookie all bent over in his corner, a phone growing out of his head, and says, "Look here. Look what I have." He then produces from his briefcase a beautiful four-color mailer. The rookie is excited. "Let me have it. I'll take 100,000 of them."

He grabs the mailer, runs to the manager's office, and, breathless, introduces this weary manager to the world of mass mailers. "Have you seen this. *Have you seen anything like this in your life?* I just ordered a hundred thousand of them. This is going to solve everything. We're going to send them to everyone in town. They'll be on light poles, under windshield wipers, in kitty litter boxes; the things will be everywhere. Everywhere! People will see them, they'll get excited, they'll clip the coupon off, staple their check to it, and mail it back to me. *Then I can do what I was really meant to do — manage money!*"

The manager, of course, has been down this path before. He looks at this rookie and says, "Sorry. We are not sending 100,000 of anything to anybody." Crestfallen, the rookie says, "Well, okay, how about 10,000?" Not that either. About that time, the wilting rookie begins to whine and says, "Can we just send 1,000?"

This wise manager does not want to completely lose this rookie — he's juiced up, he's enthusiastic, his steam is up. So he says, "Okay, who do you want to send these to?"

"Beats me," says the rookie. Enter the list salesman.

This list salesman says, "Hey, I've got a really exclusive list. But don't share this information with anybody else here. Metro area — 10,000 holders of CDs that *mature this month*. This is a superb list."

This list is so exclusive it is on a computer sheet with adhesive labels. The last person you want to be is a person on this list, because you are going to need a new postman. The one you have is going to get a hernia from carrying all that literature because 200 other rookies out there bought that list and they are sending out information as fast as they can.

The rookie whips out a thousand or so of these exclusive names and how many does he get back? Nationally, the average is about four. Not four percent . . . *just four*. Two of them will write across the face of it: "WHATEVER YOU DO DON'T CALL ME. Just mail that stuff you are supposed to mail but do not call my house ever, ever, ever."

The other two, however, will take that rookie's call or even call him, unsolicited. Of course, they have not talked to another live human being in the last year. Oh, and they have no assets; they have *never* had any assets.

Well, that didn't work out quite so well — expensive, time consuming, non-productive.

What is the next great idea we all used to go to market, a real popular one? Oh yeah, we did some seminars. We decided to get a crowd of folks together and we said, "I am going to whip them into an investing frenzy with my oratory. They'll get so excited that when I'm through I can just say 'clip those checks to the applications and just pass them forward please'."

Seminars are, to say the least, very tricky. The problem with seminars is, first, people want something for nothing — and with seminars that frequently means they want "Free Advice On How To Become a Millionaire With No Strings, Or Sales Calls, Attached." Second, you have to figure out who the right people are and how to get them there. You devise a great seminar on retirement income and half of the attendees are . . . . 25 years old. Retirement income? Retirement planning? Twenty-five-year-olds think they're going to live forever; they'll worry about retirement when they're 45.

This is not meant to be a blanket indictment of seminars; it's not that they can't or won't work. In fact, they work very well for a lot of top practicing professionals, *when they're done correctly*. Hastily arranged, poorly thought out seminars are a waste of your time. (In Chapter 8 we're going to discuss seminars that *do* work.)

Our rookie's typical experience, the skills used to "go to market," is the first piece of the wall — it's the aim that's off. The second part that's off is the target.

Choosing Your Targets

The first thing you must do is divide, or segment, the massive market out there so that you can attack better. Nearly every large objective in life can be broken down into a series of smaller objectives with their own characteristics. In this case, it's your marketplace.

You're not really marketing to "the population", are you? We need to break this marketplace into something that is not so insurmountable. It's like telling a client that he'll need $282,000 to send his newborn baby to college — that goal sounds so remote and mindboggling as to be unachievable. But if you tell him that he needs to save $2,400 a year, $200 a month, towards that goal, he'll come out of his apoplectic state.

There are many ways to segment target markets — by age, gender, zip code, social "status", profession. There's also product specialty — e.g. your golfer neighbor may be a good candidate for a limited partnership that invests in golf resort properties. I'm not suggesting that you ignore these commonsense approaches to targeting markets, but I am suggesting that if you want to drive higher revenue you have to go after the people who can give it to you.

To parapharase a remark from an Ernest Hemingway character, the rich really are different from you and me. *They have the money.*

For our purposes in talking about segmenting the broad-based market and examining both the size and the nature of the segments, we're going to base our segments on investable assets — dollars available for investment.

In the bottom of the "population pyramid" we will categorize these consumers as those with $250 to $25,000 in investable dollars. Now we must build a profile of these people to try to understand them — who they are, what they're all about, what drives their behavior. (You know these people; you either have them as clients or you have had them as clients in the past.)

Who are these people in the bottom segment of the marketplace? For one, they are wage or salary earners. They have a job somewhere with a regular stream of income of some kind. They are younger, probably less than 40, and are family- and debt-leveraged. *They are basically a processing center.* The money comes in, gets processed, gets sent back out — mortgage payments, tuition payments, car payments, grocery payments. They live for today. That's part of their family- and debt-leveraged state; they don't have a chance to plan for tomorrow yet. They also usually have minimal net-worth. Many of them may be "blue collar" households or they may be white collar twenty-somethings just starting out in life, marriage, accumulation, careers.

What about their level of financial experience and sophistication? Very low. In fact, you will even find people in this group who are very educated—medical or legal professionals — and intelligent about their businesses, but are financial neophytes.

Is this a big market or a small one? *It is huge.* There are lots of them. And it is low risk — the prospects and clients are in plentiful supply.

Are they accessible? Yes. You can call them on the phone and say, "May I speak to George, please?" George will say, "It's your dime; start talking." Are they decisive or nondecisive? They are typically very nondecisive.

Let's assume your client in this entry level of the market has eventually gotten to the point of making a decision — what criteria does he or she use? While there are two primary *reasons* that people make decisions — needs and fears — there are really only two ways that people use to arrive *at* their decisions — logic and emotion. (Psychologists tell us that some groups do a little of both: they *buy* with emotion and *justify* with logic.)

Most clients in the lower segment of the marketplace base decisions on emotion. They will ask you, "WELL . . . . HOW DO *YOU* FEEL ABOUT IT?" When this happened to me in the past, sometimes I wanted to say, "How do you *think* I feel about it? I'm trying to sell it!"

When our clients ask us how we feel about it, how do we answer? We say, "Oh, well, it's got a p/e of only 7 or a Beta of .8," or some other highly technical response. Of course, you get a blank look, because you have answered an emotional question with a logical response. And you wonder why you've lost them.

If your clients in this group ask you *how* you feel about something, they are saying to you "I make my decisions emotionally." *You* had better respond in an emotional manner . This is your clue that their only assimilation of information used to make decisions is on an emotional base. If, on the other hand, they ask you *why* you feel the way you do, then you can use the more technical data — logic. This is a request for validation of logic — use it. But if you tell them "why" you feel the way you do when they have asked you "how" you feel, you will most assuredly lose them.

A Deal That Will Double Your Income

You and I constantly get the command from "on high": SELL MORE! Always, sell more. In this lower segment of the market, how do you sell more? The first way to do that is to see more, to get more exposure. "But Les," you're saying, "there are a finite number of hours in the day, and therefore a finite number of people I can see." Right! I don't care if they are lined up outside your door with checks in hand there is only a certain number you can see and then it's over because you've run out of the 24 hours in that day.

What is the other thing you can do to sell more

in this group? (And I don't mean "reallocating and repositioning assets", as the current industry euphemism goes.) You can *close* more — get more of those you see to do business with you.

Is there a finite number of people you can close? Yes, absolutely . . . . *it's 100 percent.* You can't get more than all of them, can you? I don't care how good you are or how many years of experience you have, you just can't get more than *everybody.* Is there anybody who always gets 100 percent? Who never misses? (I've been asking professionals that question for years and I haven't found anyone yet.) You can improve your closing skills, but you will still top out at 100 percent.

If you are capped in terms of the number of people you can see, in terms of the percentage you can close, and in terms of assets to invest, and you are still not meeting the constant demand to SELL MORE, where are you? Exhausted. And you just hit the wall again.

When you've hit the wall and your manager (or your own little inner voice) is still saying SELL MORE, what is the first thing you think you must do? WORK HARDER. "That's right. I'm going to come in an hour earlier and I'm going to stay an hour later. I'll even work on Saturdays."

More, more, more. What's left of the Puritan work ethic in this country is a little inner voice whispering that we will feel better about our success if we have to exhaust ourselves to achieve it, but that isn't necessarily true. Working harder won't raise commissions; it won't drive more fees; it won't increase your billable hours. You see, you're already working hard. You would not have bought this book if you weren't already working hard and had a desire to get further ahead.

Jay Batcha is a successful investment professional with First of Michigan in Traverse City, Mich. He knows about plateaus and hard work.

"When I moved to Traverse City in 1984, right out of college, I knew absolutely no one. And I was in a city of only 40,000 people — with about 200 brokers as competition. As a rookie broker, I'd copy a couple of pages out of the phone book every morning and just dial my way through them. I'd also clip articles from newspapers and magazines and send them with a little note. I didn't even know who I was sending them to. It was very frustrating, but it was the best way to learn about working hard. I didn't have any idea what being a successful broker was all about; I also didn't know what else I'd do.

"After a year or two, my phone started ringing with calls from people I'd cold-called calling me back, or people who had saved the articles I'd sent them. After several years, I'd built up a pretty good clientele and a pretty good reputation as a stock picker and portfolio manager. Between 1985 and 1987, I went to $100,000 in gross production, but I got stuck there. I had plateaued. Then the market crashed and I was working twice as hard to do that same $100,000.

"I finally started paying attention to 'target marketing'. It made me take a long, hard look at my client book and see what was going on. I found that I had a fair number of clients who were successful business owners in the oil distribution and servicing industry. Once I'd gotten three, all of a sudden I had 23. These were my clients. They were making money in the stocks I selected and managed for them — *and they have the money.*"

I'll make a deal with you. If I guarantee to double your income in the next year will you give twice as many hours to work as you did last year? Is that possible for you to do? No. Not and stay alive. More hours and harder work isn't the answer.

You still have to figure out what is in the other part of this wall. I am suggesting to you that part of the mystery of "the wall" is your market — you are not aiming high enough. *You must move to a more upscale market.* I'm not saying you should always turn away the schoolteacher who earns $35,000 and needs help with a $2,000 IRA. After all, that person may be part of this 27-to-45 year old generation that is poised to inherit an estimated $8 trillion in wealth over the next 20 years, but if that person does suddenly become an overnight hundred-thousandaire he or she will need you even more then.

Let's look at the next segment in our broad-based market.

Let's assume this group has $25,000 to $250,000 in assets; the next has $250,000 to $1,000,000. Now, when we get to the top, these folks have $1,000,000-

plus in assets. *These are the people having tea and crumpets at the Waldorf Astoria.* So, you decide, I'm tired of fooling around down here at the bottom and I'm even going to skip over the middle; I'm going to attack right at the top because that is where the big money is.

These prospects at the top are typically over 40. They have income other than from being a wage or salary earner. Their families are pretty well grown up, paid off, and gone. They are sophisticated, inaccessible, decisive, and make decisions based on logic. (You never completely eliminate emotion but it is *not* the major force with this group.) These prospects, in short, are 180 degrees, radically different from the prospects at the bottom. Yet, remember the "attack" skills you've mastered, those developed while you were working with the lower end of the economic pyramid.

Okay, you say, I'm going to just phone this guy; after all, I've gotten pretty good at cold calling. *I've taken abuse from the best of them.*

Your first problem is that Mr. or Ms. Affluent doesn't answer his or her own phones; they typically have the lines of defense set up pretty well. On to proven tactic number two: "I'll use my glossy four-color mass mailer. That'll thrill him." What are your chances with that? He doesn't open his own mail, either, so he will never see it. Fine; on to the third tactic: I'll invite him to my seminar, the one "only for people with a million bucks to invest. $900,000 — you can't get into the room."

Here is what is holding you back — at least from this upper market. First, your skills: cold calls, mass mailers, and poor seminars don't appeal to upscale investors. Second, no "position" for yourself and no clearly defined market.

The person at the top simply does not respond to the skills you have used in the past. The way you learned to "go to market" at the lower end will not be effective at the upper end because this group does not respond to mass marketing strategies. (For that matter, the big group at the bottom isn't a homogeneous mass, either.)

You are trapped in the lower end of the market because you are using the wrong skills. You must adapt your skills *and* learn new ones if you want to market to the more affluent group. If you want to build a base at the lower end and build your business with hundreds and hundreds of small accounts because you're happy there, don't change. (Your commissions, fees, and revenue won't change either.) But if you want to increase your sales and increase your income, you must move to the upscale client. That means changing the way you approach the market — and changing what you *offer* the market.

Summary — _Chapter 1:_

• _"The wall" is only a state of mind about your markets and the skills you possess._
• _People use only two criteria for making decisions — emotion and logic. Don't answer an "emotional" question with a "logical" answer._
• _The bottom segment of the market pyramid is large, unsophisticated, accessible, and indecisive._
• _The top segment of the market pyramid is small, sophisticated, inaccessible, and decisive. Upscale asset holders do not respond well to mass marketing techniques: cold calls, mass mailings, and generic seminars._

2

DON'T SELL ME THINGS

*"Tell me who admires and loves you,
and I will tell you who you are."*

Charles-Augustin Sainte-Beuve

2

The first thing you must learn about the upscale market is to market something other than a product. *Never again market another product, plan, or service.* You are going to market something much more important, something that has more power in the marketplace than anybody's product or anybody's plan. You have to market *yourself* — who you are, what you are, what you do, how you do it. Even more important is to market *how what you do affects the prospect or client.* There's an old maxim about marketing and selling — that it is transferring a conviction from the seller to the buyer. In this case, that "conviction" is you and everything you stand for.

If your clients buy you, they will buy the products, services, or plans you offer. *If they don't buy you, it doesn't make any difference what you have "for sale."* After all, most, if not all, products or services offered by financial services professionals are interchangeable. You are not.

In a masterpiece article on marketing in the Harvard Business Review, Harvard Business School professor and marketing "guru" Theodore Levitt offers this view of the sale of the product versus the person:

"The offered products will be judged in part by who personally offers it — not just who the vendor corporation is but also who the corporation's representative is. The vendor and the vendor's representative are both inextricably and inevitably part of 'the product' that the prospect must judge before he buys. The less tangible the generic product, the more powerfully and persistently the judgment about it is shaped by the 'packaging' — how it's presented, who presents it, what's implied by metaphor, simile, symbol, and other surrogates for reality." (Reprinted by permission of the Harvard Business Review. Excerpt from "Marketing Intangible Products and Product Intangibles" by Theodore Levitt, May-June, 1981, in "The Marketing Imagination" by Theodore Levitt. New York: The Free Press, 1986. © 1981 by the President and Fellows of Harvard College: all rights reserved.)

This is the essence of marketing *yourself*, as opposed to what you have for sale. You represent whatever it is you are presenting to them — a thousand shares of a mutual fund, this fine plan, that terrific insurance policy, those comprehensive tax services. Whatever the product might be, you are the embodiment of it. To build your marketing solely around products has the potential to be disastrous — because there is no uniqueness. We all have the same products and services to sell. In order to successfully market yourself, you must build a unique identity in the prospect's mind. Think, for a minute, about the "titles" we use. What, really, is the difference in one "stockbroker" or "financial planner" or "tax attorney" and the next? If you market yourself based on a generic title, once any of these terms are "defined" by a client or prospect all who use them fall under the same definition. Being generic is neither good nor bad, it's simply ineffective, does nothing to differentiate you from others, and you *lose control.*

If you want your prospects and clients to perceive you in a unique manner based on the advantages that only you bring to the marketplace, then you must manage what they see, hear, feel, and think about as it relates to you. It is a process of controlling the data input into their brains by *marketing*, and it begins by establishing V.I.P. — visibility, image, and profile.

Who Are Those Guys, Anyway?

Visibility is being seen by strategically locating yourself where you can be observed doing the things that relate to your target market. In other words, figure out where your market spends its time and *be there.*

"I make golf part of my business."

Everybody who loves the game of golf would love to chase that little white ball a day or two a week. You can — and you should — if you do it like Brian Lee, who made the above statement. Eight years ago, Brian, a top investment professional with Janney Montgomery Scott in Allentown, Penn., was an 18 handicap golfer; today he's a 3. He's worked on his golf game while working on his prospects.

"I learned a while back to use my sports background in marketing myself," he says. "Golf has enabled me to open new doors. When you take a prospect to play golf — maybe it's someone that a current client has referred to you — if you go at it from the standpoint of a mutual playing field, you will forge a bond. Somewhere over the course of 18 holes of golf you will make, *in one way or another*, your positioning statement to this prospect.

"When I play in a golf tournament, I want to be one of those guys who walks up there to collect the prize. It helps give me the aura of a winner. I want people to ask, 'Who is this Brian Lee fellow?' That's my visibility."

This year Brian, in conjunction with a local firemen's association, will put on his first golf tournament. The proceeds, about $10,000, will send burned children to camp.

"Who's going to tell me that this kind of exposure and visibility is a bad thing?" Brian asks. Who indeed.

In order to become in your prospects' minds the unique person that offers what they want, you have to create visibility for yourself. The upscale investor, in particular, will not do business with you unless he sees you acting in a manner which reinforces his idea about who he wants as a professional advisor.

Mirror, Mirror On The Wall

Let's talk about your image. In his best-selling book "How To Sell Yourself," Joe Girard, "world's greatest salesman" according to "The Guinness Book of Records," begins his discussion of selling yourself to others with some simple, almost laughable, "rules." After all, says Girard, "contents and wrapping should go hand in hand."(copyright © 1979 by Joe Girard. Reprinted by permission of Simon & Schuster, Inc.)
The rules?

- Shower or bathe daily.
- Take care of your hair.
- Use makeup sparingly (if you're a woman).
- Shave as often as necessary (if you're a man).
- Keep your nails clean, trimmed, and manicured.

- Keep physically trim.
- Check your posture.

About now, you're probably snickering and saying, Les, get serious. I am. Don't *ever* forget that your "wrapping" is important.

What do your prospects "see" when they see you? What do you look like? Dress like? Act like? Talk like? Do you look like someone so conservative that you can't beat CD rates? Do you look like someone so speculative that you might lose all your prospect's money? The image you project must meet the expectations of the group of people you wish to serve. What do they *expect* you to look like? This is a critical point because that is the image that must be achieved.

In the wonderful movie "Working Girl," a young woman working as a sales assistant in a brokerage firm wants to become a broker. She goes back to school and gets her securities license but "they" won't let her play. After transferring to another department, she finally gets her chance, but first she cuts her hair, changes her style of dress, changes her make-up, even changes her diction. "If I am going to be big time," she says, "I have to look big time."

Your **profile** is what your prospect comes to believe about you before the selling begins — and it is based on visibility and image. If you define yourself merely as "a broker" or a "financial professional" you are opening yourself up to elaboration, so to speak, of that definition by others — remember our example of "Joker vs. Broker" from Money magazine? Don't let others, particularly the media, define you.

You must manage this whole process — where you are seen, what you look like, what you talk like, what you act like and, ultimately, how your clients come to define you. *You* control the marketing of you — through your position.

Perception vs. Reality

In their highly acclaimed book "Positioning: The Battle For Your Mind," marketing consultants Al Ries and Jack Trout present the concept of positioning. It is, quite simply, "not to create something new and different, but to manipulate what's already up there in the [prospect's] mind, to retie the connections that already exist." (Al Ries and Jack Trout, "Positioning: The Battle For Your Mind," © 1981, 1986, McGraw-Hill, Inc., used with permission.)

Furthermore, say Ries and Trout, "to be successful today, you must touch base with reality. And the only reality that counts today is what's already in the prospect's mind."

Positioning, a major component of your marketing efforts, turns on your establishing a "position niche" in your prospect's mind that reflects not only *your* strengths and weaknesses but those of your competitors as well. Don't ever forget that you *are* marketing against everyone else.

Ries and Trout also offer these thoughts on marketing against competitors. (Al Ries and Jack Trout, "Bottom-Up Marketing," © 1989, McGraw-Hill, Inc., used with permission):

"The great myth of marketing is that 'serving the customer' is the name of the game. Many marketing people live in a dream world. They believe in the fantasy of the virgin market. This is the belief that marketing is a two-player game involving just the company and the customer. In this fantasy, a company develops a product or service designed to appeal to consumer needs and wants and then uses marketing to harvest the crop.

"There are no virgin markets. The reality of marketing is that a market consists of consumers strongly or weakly held by a range of competitors."

Marketing Revolutions and Evolutions

Prior to and just after World War II, marketing was product driven. It was basically built on this principle: "This is what this product *is* and if you need one come on down to 4th and Main. We have them." It was the better mousetrap days — before more and *better* better mousetraps flooded the market.

Marketing then became consumer driven: "This is what this product *does* — for you — and if you need one come on down to 4th and Main. We have something that can do that for you."

Consumer driven marketing was followed by the image-driven era, masterminded by legendary adman David Ogilvy, founder of the New York ad agency Ogilvy & Mather.

During the latter half of the '80s and now into the '90s, marketing has become competitor driven: *how your prospects see you versus the alternatives available to them.* In the financial services business, in particular, it is no longer a situation of choice — of whether people want to have financial services or not. They *have* to have them. This principle applies to other professional services—such as legal, accounting, and medical—as well. The ultimate marketing decision in the '90s is *who,* not *whether.* Your marketing efforts must now be competitor driven — you must position and identify yourself in a unique fashion to fulfill the prospect's needs and wants, even if that person fails to know what they are.

Let's look briefly at a classic example of competitor driven-marketing.

Who is the number one automobile rental firm in the world? Hertz. Who is number two — and says they are? Avis. What does Avis say about themselves? "We try harder." What does that imply about Hertz? *That maybe they don't try so hard?*

"WE TRY HARDER." The implication is that they will hustle harder, provide cleaner cars, quicker service — do things better to get and keep your business. Now, their newest campaign: "Talk to the owner." *(Because at Hertz you can't?)* Avis clearly positions itself against the alternative.

When prospects ask you, "What do you do?," how do you answer them? You probably say, "I am a financial planner," or "I am a CPA," or "I am a stockbroker," or some other generic term that has a pre-existing definition in the prospect's mind.

They haven't asked "what are you?" "What do you do?" is different from "what are you?," and the marketplace doesn't really care what you "are." More specifically, the prospect wants to know "what do you *do* as it relates to *me*, the prospect?" The way you answer this question is critical to your marketing success.

Let me give you an example that illustrates people's preconceived ideas of "what you do" versus " what you are" and how that can be changed for more positive acceptance.

A couple of years ago, I was scheduled to make a presentation to a major brokerage office in Philadelphia. I arrived at the office about 8:00 a.m. so I'd have plenty of time to set up before our 9:00 a.m. starting time. At that hour, *nobody* is at the reception desk of a brokerage office. I walked in with my load of things, looked around, saw no one, and just hollered out, "Anybody here?" Out from the back comes this fellow with this rig over his head — headset and microphone, cord hanging down his back. I had just stumbled onto an early morning cold call cowboy — this guy could have one hand on the quote machine and one on the telephone and rock and roll all day long. I later learned that this broker does about $800,000 in gross commissions, so he does what he does *very* well. (One thing he does very well is reach small business owners in the early morning hours — a time when they're not distracted by the rest of the day's business.)

He asked if he could help me. I told him that I was with a major mutual fund company and was there to do a program that day for some of the brokers. He made some nice comments about a mutual fund which he had sold for a number of years, and then said, "What product are you here to talk about?"

He had just made an assumption about me — that I was a product vendor. I said, "I am not here to talk about a product." Then, with a look of surprise on his face, came the ultimate question: "What do you do?"

I could have answered him from *my* point of view. I could have said, "I teach marketing; I teach sales." Or, "I'm a motivational speaker." But at $800,000 gross commission income this broker did not need motivating!

What do I know that all brokers, planners, accountants, agents, and other professionals want more of? *Money.* They will do strange and unusual things to get it: brokers will call perfect strangers on the phone and say, "Send me a hundred thousand dollars," and fully believe they are going to get it. What's weird is *sometimes they do.*

Knowing from my "profile" of this broker that he is paid by commission and that he would like even *more* commissions — understanding what drives his behavior — I said to him, "I travel the country for my company, working with professionals in financial services, doubling their commissions."

That broker followed me to the conference room and helped me set up. I even thought he was going to follow me into the men's room. What would make him follow me around like that? $1.6 million, that's what. No other driving force.

You see, *I identified what I do with what he wanted to have happen.* He wanted $1.6 million a year in gross commissions to happen. People don't really want to "buy" stocks, bonds, annuities, insurance plans, or legal services. They want what these things *do* for them.

Consider this enlightening example from the book "How To Win Customers and Keep Them For Life." (Michael LeBoeuf, Ph.D., "How to Win Customers and Keep them For Life," © 1987, Michael LeBoeuf, Berkley Books/The Berkley Publishing Group, used with permission.) He relates this plea from an "anonymous customer":

"Don't sell me clothes. Sell me a sharp appearance, style, and attractiveness.

Don't sell me insurance. Sell me peace of mind and a great future for my family and me.

Don't sell me a house. Sell me comfort, content-
ment, a good investment, and pride of ownership.
Don't sell me books. Sell me pleasant hours
and the profits of knowledge.
Don't sell me toys. Sell my children happy mo-
ments.
Don't sell me a computer. Sell me the pleasures
and profits of the miracles of modern technology.
Don't sell me tires. Sell me freedom from worry
and low cost per mile.
Don't sell me airline tickets. Sell me a fast, safe,
on-time arrival at my destination feeling like a million dollars.
Don't sell me things. Sell me ideals, feelings,
self-respect, home life, and happiness.
Please don't sell me *things.*"

It's the same with your prospects. They don't
care what you are and what you have to sell. They
care about what you do — from *their* perspective.
In your prospect's mind that question always
looms. Before you can answer this question you
must establish a profile about *this* client or prospect,
much of which can be done through simple logic
and deductive reasoning. Here's a sample prospect
profile.
Your prospect is 72 years old. He has $400,000
in assets, his home is paid for, and his only other
source of income is Social Security. What does this
client want? His first concern is safety. What does
he have to have? A "must have" requirement is an

adequate income stream. The question in his mind is: what do you do? *Oh, I'm a stockbroker/financial planner/insurance agent.* That ought to really ring his chimes.

Try this "position" instead: "I design and implement programs that can provide high retirement income in a predictable fashion." You have now described in his terms what you do.   This should, at the very least, arouse some curiosity. *"OH? HOW DO YOU DO THAT?"* Your prospect has just opened up his mind to let you in.

Only through strong positioning can you get your prospects to let you in and listen to what you have to say. Once they have "opened up" you can use the good selling skills you already have in place — if you have marketed yourself properly with positioning and uniquely identified yourself in their minds.

Summary — Chapter 2:

• *If your clients buy you they will buy the products, plans, or services you offer.*

• *There is no "uniqueness" in building your marketing around products — we all have the same products to sell.*

• *Visibility, image, and profile lead to your position.*

• *Marketing in the '90s is competitor-driven — how your prospects see you versus the alternatives available to them.*

• *Your clients and prospects care about only one thing — what you do from their perspective.*

3

GETTING THE BEACHHEAD:
Lessons from Eisenhower to Schwarzkopf

"For all your days prepare,
And meet them ever alike:
When you are the anvil, bear —
When you are the hammer, strike."

Edwin Markham, "The Gates of Paradise
and Other Poems"

3

Your task as a professional services practitioner is to identify the strategic skills you need to create a unique difference between you and your competitors. This will help you attack the marketplace. But before you learn more about attacking, you must understand how the principles of war can have a major impact on your success — or lack thereof.

There is a relatively obscure book (unless you're a student of the military), a thorough study of warfare, that is a classic in its examination of the various facets of conflict. "On War," the memoirs of Carl Von Clausewitz, was published by his wife after his death.

Carl Von Clausewitz, born in 1780, became a second lieutenant in the Prussian army in 1792 at 12 years old. The military became his entire life. During his career in the Prussian armed forces, he observed many of Napoleon's campaigns and became a chronicler of great military battles, as well as a general. His curiosity spurred him to explore war in all its detail. Is there a commonality about defeat?

Are there issues about battles and war that will remain constant? Are there certain principles that must be adhered to before a state can engage in warfare?

Clausewitz says that, "War is nothing but a duel on an extensive scale. If we would conceive as a unit the countless number of duels which make up a War, we shall do so best by supposing to ourselves two wrestlers. Each strives by physical force to compel the other to submit to his will: each endeavours to throw his adversary, and thus render him incapable of further resistance. War therefore is an act of violence intended to compel our opponent to fulfil our will." (Carl Von Clausewitz, "On War," edited by Anatol Rapoport, Penguin Books 1968, introduction and notes © Penguin Books, 1968, reproduced by permission of Penguin Books Ltd.)

War — opposition, conquest, occupation, submission, victory. Or defeat.

How can an understanding of the nature and principles of war be instrumental in marketing? Marketing consultants Al Ries and Jack Trout were the first to introduce the concept of applying the principles of war to the "real world" and the first to present these principles in layman's language. In their book "Marketing Warfare" they offer this more contemporary definition of war and its application to the consumer marketplace (Al Ries and Jack Trout, "Marketing Warfare," © 1986, McGraw-Hill, Inc., used with permission):

"Marketing battles are not fought in the customer's office or in the supermarkets or the drugstores of America. Those are only distribution points for the merchandise whose brand selection is decided elsewhere. Marketing battles are not fought in places like Dallas, Detroit, or Denver. At least not in the physical sense of a city or a region.

"Marketing battles are fought in a mean and ugly place. A place that's dark and damp with much unexplored territory and deep pitfalls to trap the unwary. Marketing battles are fought inside the mind. Inside your own mind and inside the mind of your prospects, every day of the week.

"The mind is the battleground. A terrain that is tricky and difficult to understand. The entire battleground is just 6 inches wide. This is where the marketing war takes place. You try to outmaneuver and outfight your competitors on a mental mountain about the size of a canteloupe.

"A marketing war is a totally intellectual war with a battleground that no one has ever seen. It can only be imagined in the mind, which makes marketing warfare one of the most difficult disciplines to learn."

Marketing is all about *the conquest and occupation of the human mind,* about capturing and holding a territory, an identity, inside the head of a target group you wish to serve. This is the battlefield. You must "take" a certain piece of ground inside a prospect's head and create your identity — beliefs about you, your products, and your company — *before* selling starts.

Let's examine some of Clausewitz's principles of war as they relate to marketing.

Principle #1: Wouldn't It Be Nice If... vs. Let's Do It

The **first principle of war is setting the objective** — you must decide what it is you wish to do. This concept of establishing a predetermined objective is critical — and powerful. In 1961, in his inaugural address, President John F. Kennedy said, "We're going to put a man on the moon by the end of this decade." July, 1969, Neil Armstrong walked on the moon. What do you think the difference would have been if he had said, "Wouldn't it be nice, *wouldn't it be great*, if *someday* we could put a man on that moon."

Objective-setting is so powerful, in fact, that inferior forces who have a clear objective can occasionally defeat superior forces who lack a strong and true objective. Remember from your history lessons how 300 Spartans held off 20,000 Persians at Thermopylae? How, for nearly a week, 200 Texans held off the Marquis de Santa Ana and 2,000 Mexicans at the Alamo? Remember another classic battle, a bloody conflict in the U.S. from 1860 to

1865? The Civil War or The War Between the States.

What was the Southern army's objective? Did they want to conquer or occupy the North, imposing their way of life on the rest of the country? No. They just wanted those Northerners to go away and leave them alone. Their objective was *military* — to play defense. With a clearly defined objective, the Southern army was able to hold off a Union force that was vastly superior in numbers for quite awhile.

What was President Abraham Lincoln's objective — military or political? In 1861 Lincoln was faced with ethnic unrest, slavery, and economic chaos from a patchwork of onerous taxes and tariffs. Individual states were declaring themselves separate from the Union. (We've seen this recently in the former Soviet Union and Yugoslavia.)

Mr. Lincoln decided that he would use force to hold the Union together. He gathered up his large Northern army and said, in effect, "You men go South and get them straightened out." With the massive strength of the North, who would have thought the war would take four years and over 600,000 lives.

Despite this *tactical* use of force, Lincoln's initial *objective* was *political* — to preserve the Union: "You elected me President of this Union and it is not going to fall apart while I am in office." In 1863, more than two years after the beginning of the war, Lincoln issued a political document, the Emancipation Proclamation, which had the effect of charging the army with a *military* objective—to free men. It also welded the will of the people together. He then hired a hard-headed, whiskey-drinking Yankee by the name of Ulysses S. Grant, who looked around and discovered the North had a 9-to-1 advantage in troop strength. He then began to *act* on the new military objective.

Principle #2: Make Force Your Friend

With a clear objective in place, the **second principle of war — force — can be used to advantage**. Quite simply put, the most powerful wins. As far as you are concerned force is all about creating the dominant position in your predetermined target markets. Just as in warfare the most powerful force usually wins, so it is in markets.

Think for a minute about who is the dominant player in providing "financial services" in most major metropolitan areas. It's your friendly banker, whose overriding "position" is: "WE ARE SAFE." Do you sell anything that's as safe as the bank? Yes, you do — it's called a brokered CD or government bond. But . . . will the client ever really believe in his or her heart that the CD he or she buys from you is as safe as the one at the bank? NO. You and I know it's the same thing, but in the client's reality, it is not. In the client's mind, there is a difference, and the *client's reality* is that with which you have to deal.

For you to get force to work in your favor, to be your friend rather than your enemy, you must segment the marketplace into small, manageable entities that allow you to have a dominant position in that marketplace. If you use demographics to define your markets carefully, there will be no "gray" areas.

Several years ago, I was involved in conducting a number of interviews with top brokers and planners, those with million dollar-plus gross commission income. My colleagues and I asked them, "How, indeed, do you segment this big market out there? How do you get a handle on what you want to do and to whom you want to market?"

These successful professionals unanimously named two keys to their success. The first was segmentation. All these major players did not serve a broad base; they had very small, well-defined targets. We then asked them about the size market they feel is best. Their answer may surprise you: the optimal size for a target market is *200 people*, tops. It may even be smaller, but should not exceed 200 on a per-campaign basis.

I've done some work with three brokers in the Midwest, a three-man partnership that produces about $1.1 million a year. Not bad, right? But they have 4,700 accounts. Can you guess how many outgoing phone calls this office makes each year between January 1st and April 15th? None. They're too busy answering phone calls from the dormant account-holder who asks, "What is my cost basis on that $5,000 mutual fund I bought two years ago?" You get the picture. We looked closely at their book of business and determined that over 2,000 of those accounts had not generated *any* income for at least three years. None. Several clients were deceased!

On the other hand, I know a broker in the Southeast who has only 147 accounts. He manages $410 million, all in wrap accounts — one percent a year, every year, on $410 million. Which book of business would you rather have?

Nearly all successful practicing professionals I know have clearly defined, extremely targeted segments of the market, but when I describe these successful professionals and their target markets of 200 people, other professionals look at me like I'm crazy. You may even be saying to yourself, "Only 200? I'll be out of business." Probably not. Unlike the rookie who sends out 1,000 pieces of mail hoping to get a handful back, when you narrow your segment down to 100 or 150 or 200 *you want them all.* Every single one of them. You want to dominate that segment and gain possession of their minds and their assets.

Jay Batcha, the successful First of Michigan broker, probably "owns" the active- and retired-oil executive marketplace in Traverse City, Mich. That actually may be only 30 people, but if Jay has 23 you'd probably agree that he is the dominant player.

"I don't necessarily point out to people 'I work with oil executives', but it is definitely an active network," Jay says. "They all talk to each other."

Two hundred per proactive, outgoing campaign. Maybe, like Jay Batcha, all you need is 30.

Saying that you need a small target market doesn't necessarily mean you can't have more than one. Brian Lee, our successful golfer-investment advisor, is a great example of a professional with a "split book." Brian lives and works in Allentown, Penn. But, every month, he manages a substantial number of assets for Connecticut residents.

Connecticut? Isn't that a several-hour drive from Allentown?

Several years ago, Brian was referred to a person in Fairfield County, Conn. (just outside New York City), where Brian grew up, who had been an insurance client of his father's. Brian drove up to see this prospect and, as luck and good marketing skills would have it, this prospect gave Brian the largest single stock purchase order he had ever received.

"One day not long after the trip and the trade," Brian says, "the executive vice president of branch management called me and said, 'Was your trip successful?'. I said, 'Yes, great'. He said, 'Then why the hell aren't you back up there? Why aren't you going up every month?'"

Six years later there are clients in Connecticut who hold on to checks waiting for Brian to come up — *they know he'll be there.* Brian has recently carved out another target market, also in Connecticut. He is now working with a group of about 40 CPAs and tax attorneys, consulting with them on their clients' investment plan implementations. *They know he'll be there.*

"I've got target markets all over the place," says Brian. Small, specific, targeted groups.

Principle #3: Did Schwarzkopf Really Play Offense?

Principle of war number three is the superiority of defense. Playing defense is actually easier than offense. When General Norman Schwarzkopf, hero of the Persian Gulf war, was challenged by the press — "Why don't you attack?" — he quoted Clausewitz: you must have a 3-to-1 tactical advantage on offense.

What does this mean to you, the financial professional? It is easier to keep accounts on the books and clients in your practice — and to get additional money from those people — than to get new ones. Every account you have has more money and more needs. Planners, agents, brokers, and accountants ask me all the time as I travel around the country, "How can I get some business *right now*? I need some quickly." Don't we all. The quickest way to get more business right now is to go to your client book — attack the top 25 percent and get *all* of their assets. Don't leave any out there.

Principle #4: This Isn't Football

Attack or defend; which should you do? **Principle number four says you must do both** — if you are going to be successful.

Successful marketing isn't like football, in which you can run one team on, a whistle blows, everybody stops, and you can put another team on — offense, defense, or special teams. It is like basketball — up and down, offense and defense, back and forth, all at the same time. You must attack an account to get new business and you must defend the existing positions you have.

Clearly, the first critical element of attack and defend is that objective we discussed earlier — defining a clear and attainable goal — and to support that objective you must develop certain tactical skills. This requires understanding your strengths and weaknesses and then using them to maximum advantage in your marketing campaigns. From this tactical base you can then build a strategy that is appropriate.

Begin with an assessment of the skills you have developed as a practicing professional — *use* the good skills you have and *get better* at the ones that are weak. If you're not a good public speaker, don't get involved in public speaking. If you're an excellent "wordsmith", think about writing some articles for publication. If you're less than effective on the telephone, don't crank up a cold call campaign.

Your skills are as different as you are. Put your good ones to good use.

To be effective on the attack you must also be bold — you need to become a rule-breaker. I don't mean NASD, SEC, or other legal or regulatory rules that apply to your specific business, not your company's rules, not even your own office's rules, but *the rules you have put on yourself.*

You have harnessed yourself with some "rules": "I just do bonds." "I only do annuities." "I only sell whole life." Oh really? Then if your client says to you that he wants to buy 10,000 shares of IBM or a $2 million term insurance policy are you telling me you won't take the check? Where are all those financial service professionals from the early '80s who "only did tax shelters?" That kind of approach is *not* identifying a target group and being responsive to its needs, and, as we've discussed before, to "identify" yourself based on a product is simply suicidal. Break a few rules.

While you are on the attack remember another critical element — mass your forces and stay directed. In warfare, rare is the divided army that can be successful. It must stay massed in order to preserve its power. In your own marketing warfare, if you remain directed and focused on the target market at hand, you will become *market driven* and *market identified*. When you begin to get 15 or 20 percent of a target market, you will begin to be recognized as the vendor of choice to those people, whoever they are: *"You'd better talk to Bob Smith at*

Omnipotent Investments because he's the only one who understands automobile dealers — how we operate and what we need."

Remember Jay Batcha's comments about the business owners in the oil industry? "Once I had three, all of a sudden I had 23."

Finally, in your marketing attack, you must attack on a narrow front. Once you determine the need or desire that *drives this target market* attack there, and only there, with all force. Is your target market (200 people, remember?) concerned primarily with planning for their children's college? Pre-retirement options? Post-retirement income streams? Tax minimization? Once you're in, then go after the rest of it, but if you can't get in, the rest doesn't matter.

June 6, 1944. D-day. Adolf Hitler had four, maybe five, times more troops on the continent than General Dwight Eisenhower. Who won? Did you ever wonder how?

Maybe as you recall history lessons you'd say Ike had "better guys" — a better trained, more disciplined, superior army. No; there may never have been a better army than Hitler's troops in World War II. Better armor and artillery, you say? No again. There's never been better armor than what the Germans had. If Hitler had a better army with better armor and better positions how exactly did Ike win? It wasn't surprise—Hitler knew there were a million and a half men on the island of Great Britain, and he certainly knew they were coming to the continent, not exactly where or when but he knew they were going to show up.

Ike had a **single, clearly defined goal**. It wasn't "take all of Europe;" it was simply *get on the beach and stay there*. He had to have the **tactical skills** to make that happen and he had to **be bold**, to break some rules. Why would the Germans believe Eisenhower would never try to come on shore at Normandy? Well, there are huge reefs that lie just under the surface, seriously inhibiting supply and support ships' access to the beach. It was *impossible*; German logic said it could *not* be done. But several days after D-Day, there were huge crafts moored out at the reefs spilling out everything needed to continue to fuel the army and the attack — a virtual floating port. One hundred and fifty-six thousand men stormed ashore on a small strip of beach. Operation Overlord had begun.

On that day, Ike didn't have better men or better equipment, but he had **more of them right at the unexpected point of attack**. It wasn't a massive force; it didn't grow to the million troops needed for a major campaign on the continent until days later. It started with that little stretch of beach at Normandy.

Ike didn't try to take it all at once; he figured out the small part he could take, and then expanded. *He got the beachhead first*. It's the same with your marketing efforts: decide on your objective, use the skills you have, mass your strength, stay directed — and get a small beachhead.

Now that we've discussed some examples of the attack portion of the fourth principle of war — attack-and-defend — we must turn to defending.

Championship Games Are Won With Defense

As surely as you are sitting there reading this book, your major competitors are calling on your prospects and clients, desperately trying to take them away from you. If you play good defense, you won't lose them.

As with defining the objective on the attack, the first, critical element in playing good defense is to define what must be defended. If you think this sounds simplistic or trite, think about your clients for a minute. Frankly, you've probably got a few clients and accounts you wish somebody would take away from you, but there are also some that are precious and valuable and too dear to lose. You must know who these people are before you can define their value to your business.

The second step in playing good defense is to identify and develop the skills necessary to defend your client base — e.g. what is absolutely critical on your part to keep your clients with you? Finally, you must have the courage to attack yourself. Let me illustrate this point with a personal story.

In 1977 I was in the consulting business in Winston-Salem, N.C. In consulting, someone has to sell the new business, someone has to deliver the service, and someone has to administer the project. As a consultant, if you're the seller of the business you usually get 25 percent of the face value of the contract. If you write the program, actually deliver the service, you get another 25 percent of the contract. In some cases, I was both the salesperson and the consultant assigned to the project.

That year, I sold a large training contract to a major power company in the Southeast that would last four years. The account would pay me a substantial sum of money for selling the business and since I would also deliver the service I would receive another large sum. It was most definitely an account you'd fight to defend.

One day, my boss called me to his office and said, "Les, we have a problem. Your biggest account just called, cancelled the contract, and said they don't ever want to do business with us again. I'd like for you to go to your office." I thought he was going to tell me to clean out my desk, but instead he told me to write a list of reasons as to why I thought this client would have cancelled. I didn't go — I slithered, with my tail tucked in.

Well, I worked on my list, went back to my boss, and said, "Here are the things I can think of that would have caused them to fire us: I failed to give them a report after the third training group, I moved the training location, changed the dates, changed some of the material in the manual . . . and there may have been a few other things."

He looked over my list and then said, "Les, I have to be honest with you." Oh no, I thought, here comes my pink slip. "Your biggest account didn't call us and they didn't fire us. *But if you don't go do these things, they will.*"

Attack yourself. What are you doing that you shouldn't be doing? What are you not doing that you should be doing? Why are your clients not doing more business with you?

The most powerful way to attack yourself is to take a long, hard look at your 20 or 30 most valuable clients and pretend they aren't yours. What would you have to do to get them? What could you deliver to them that they are not now receiving? I can guarantee that if you can figure out a way to get these accounts, or get them back, your competitors can also figure out a way.

To determine whether you're doing the right things to defend this business, start by *asking your clients*. That may sound pretty basic, but have you said to a valued client lately, "Is there anything you'd like to have done that I'm not doing for you?"

It's amazing how a simple little question like that may get you an answer like, "Actually, yes, I need to set up a pension and profit sharing plan for my business." *But since all you do are mutual funds I didn't know you could do that . . . .*

William I. ("Bill") Kissinger, CPA, CFP, a successful veteran of the financial services profession who is president of Kissinger Financial Services, Inc., in Timonium, Md., says that playing good defense means being constantly responsive to your clients' changing needs.

"When we've lost clients over the years, and we have, just like everyone else, it was because we didn't do a good enough job in their care and feeding," Bill says. "We deserved to lose them." Bill, who has only about 190 clients, is an ardent believer in the "limited client" philosophy.

"I hear other practicing professionals talk about having 600 clients. That's baloney. Maybe that's how many trade confirmations are in the file. Those are *not* clients."

Bill believes that the true definition of a client is someone with whom he and his staff have an ongoing relationship. For Kissinger Financial, that means specifically a person who is paying him an on-going monitoring fee, in addition to commissioning a financial plan and investment implementation. "We want clients who are committed to this type relationship," Bill says.

There's a simple lesson here: increased services to the client should result in increased revenues for you. You're not in business for your health.

For Bill and his associates, getting more business from current clients — *defending* the client relationship — amounts to what he calls a "one stop shopping" approach. He had so many clients over the years ask his advice on mortgages that Kissinger Financial now serves as a mortgage banker, too. Mortgage banking? *I thought all you did was mutual funds . . . .*

"The 'old attitudes' in this business went like this: 'it's not my job to sell you an insurance policy. Or, 'I don't want to pick stocks and bonds'. But you have to make your goal finding out what the client wants," Bill says. "Our 'new values' mean we can't, and won't, be dedicated in our clients' eyes to one product. It's too big a risk and you don't serve the client's needs." Good defense.

One of the reasons the Eisenhower-led attack at Normandy was so successful was that there was no strong defense. The German high command got together once a week and played war games, appointing one guy to be Eisenhower. They knew all about the men Eisenhower had, the route he might take, where he might come ashore (Port of Calais, the obvious choice). Their defense was ready — or so they thought. *Nobody* would *ever* attack at Normandy. It was ludicrous to think that anybody would select that part of the continent's coast. Surprise.

Principle #5: Along The Banks Of The San Jacinto

There is one **last principle of war** with which you must become intimate: you must **choose the battlefield.** *You* select the criteria on how this attack-and-defend process will take place.

Everybody remembers the Marquis de Santa Ana for his decisive Alamo victory with 2,000 men over 200 rag-tag Texans and Tennesseeans. With those odds, you wouldn't think that battle would have lasted long at all, but the Alamo didn't fall for several days.

After Santa Ana was finished in San Antonio, he headed east, looking for Sam Houston. Houston gathered up a motley group of soldiers and headed west to meet Santa Ana along the banks of the San Jacinto River. Houston managed to "lose" a couple of strategic skirmishes, at the same time drawing Santa Ana in, and then turning his limited artillery loose, he destroyed the Mexican army. He decided where and how to fight. He chose the battlefield.

For you, dictating the terms of battle means selecting and controlling the criteria that the prospect uses to arrive at the decision: who's going to provide me with the services I need? If you can control the *process*, you can control the outcome of the *decision*.

Summary — Chapter 3:

• *Marketing is the conquest and occupation of the human mind. This is the battlefield.*
• *The first principle of war and marketing is to set the objective — a critical and powerful concept.*
• *The second principle of war is force. That means creating a dominant position in your target markets.*
• *Superiority of defense, the third principle of war, means it is easier to keep clients and get more of their business than it is to get new clients.*
• *The fourth principle of war dictates that, to be successful in your target markets, you must both attack and defend.*
• *Good defense means having the courage to attack yourself — what are you not doing for your clients that you should be doing?*
• *The last principle of war is to choose the battlefield — you select the criteria for the attack-and-defend strategy.*

4

WHY YOU?

"We won't be deceived
by titles such as Indispensable and Unique and
Great.
Someone else indispensable and unique and great
Can always be found at a moment's notice."

Constantine Cavafy,
"When The Watchman Saw The Light"

4

In 1974 I returned to school, entering the MBA program at Wake Forest University. It was probably the most frightening experience of my life.

I say that in spite of the fact that, during my tour of duty in Vietnam with the Marine Corps, I was shot down, shot at, and overrun by the army of North Vietnam. You see, I was a forward observer for mortars and artillery along the demilitarized zone for 15 months, so I saw some pretty horrifying things. When I went to Vietnam, I was 22 years old, had been in the Corps for nearly three years, and was as well prepared as a young man could be for what I was about to face. I was not, however, prepared to go back to school, largely because of my experience as an undergraduate.

In undergraduate school I could never quite reconcile in my mind why anyone in his right mind would spend good "socializing" money on textbooks; it just didn't make sense to me. I thought that I could pass nearly every course offered in college without actually buying the books required. If you think about the way we are taught and the way we learn, it makes sense. You can pass a math course if you absorb what the professor tells you, record it in your mind, and give it right back to him.

I owned a total of six books in undergraduate school, including none for history courses, a subject in which I never made less than an A. I certainly read a lot — I still do — and I made a point of reading many books that were and are helpful to me, but I never owned a history textbook.

Now that you have a feel for my undergraduate academic "philosophy," if you will, you can understand why I felt unprepared to face the rigors of graduate school, particularly a demanding school like Wake Forest University.

The second year of the MBA program has a required course in marketing. At that point, I had been in the direct sales and sales management business for seven years, opening and managing sales organizations all around the country. *I knew something about marketing.*

The bio sheet on the professor for my marketing course indicated that he had received his undergraduate degree from the University of Buffalo. His MBA was from the University of Buffalo, as was his Ph.D. He had had a teaching fellowship at the University of Buffalo and was also an associate professor at . . . the University of Buffalo. That was the sum total of his academic credentials and experience.

I read this and said to myself, hmmm, this guy's

going to teach me marketing — but he's never been out there and faced customers, he's never been out of academia, for that matter he's never been out of *Buffalo!* What does he know about marketing?

I decided to have a little chat with the Dean about my misgivings concerning this professor. I said to him, "Look, I'm right off the streets; I've been out here doing this marketing stuff for a living. I know what it's all about because I've faced customers. I want some stimulation." The Dean convinced me to "stay with the program" (it was either that or a home study program that would have *really* been a challenge), and so I went to class, not expecting much.

On the first day of class, I was sitting way up in the peanut gallery of this large amphitheater when in walks the professor, all 6 foot 6 inches and 350 pounds of him, with a full bushy beard, long shaggy hair, and double knit pants. He began class by announcing, "I understand we have a marketing expert in our class. Mr. Anderson, would you please stand up." He asked me this question: "How many ways can a product or service, any product or service, appeal to buyers, any buyer, in a marketplace, any marketplace?"

As had been my modus operandi in the past, I began thinking with my mouth open — it gets me into trouble every time I do it. I responded thusly: "It would seem to me that every individual, each and every one of us, could be a market unto himself or herself." He agreed. "There's 210 million of us in this country; ergo, the potential for 210 million markets." He agreed again. "There's thousands upon thousands of products and services, so if I multiply that times 210 million potential markets, we're talking about a pretty good sized number. I guess the appeal is infinite." Some conclusion. The professor said, "Well, Mr. Anderson, you were doing pretty good until you got to your conclusion and that demonstrates to me that you really don't know that much about marketing. Though I only have eight months with you, if you'll sit down and be quiet from here on out, I'll do my best to try to teach you a little something about marketing."

He did. I learned a lot about markets and products and their appeal to buyers; I learned that there are really only four "rungs" on the product/service ladder of appeal, as nearly all marketing texts will tell you.

All Things Being Equal . . . .

The first way that a product or service can appeal to a buyer in a marketplace is when product or service "A" is *equal* to product or service "B." If your client buys 1,000 shares of XYZ Mutual Fund from you or from your colleague across town, what's the difference in what the client owns when the transaction is complete? Nothing. You sell the same products, services, or advice as any other financial professional.

That being the case, how does a person select a vendor? If the product or service is identical, the **first buying criteria is price.** It is the "raw cost" — e.g. is one cheaper than another? If the price, however, is also identical — a mutual fund no matter who the vendor is — then **the second buying criteria, delivery,** becomes a deciding factor. (Many people are tempted to say "service", but you only find out about service *after* the sale. Service is frequently the reason for the second, third, or fourth sale, but not necessarily the first.) Delivery, or the delivery/distribution system is, simply, whether your prospect can get it as easily from the next person as from you.

The delivery buying criteria is made up of two key elements — **availability and incumbency.** The latter — the relationship that was in place prior to your coming on the scene — is a powerful force that frequently results in a strong bond between buyer and seller. Despite the turnover at the highest level in our most recent national election, the percentage of incumbents who are re-elected, from dogcatcher to city council member to senator, is historically very high — usually over 90 percent. Put another way, the odds are 9-1 against you unseating a relationship already in place.

When price and delivery combine in such a way that "all things are equal," the sale, as well as the buying decision, emulates that of a commodity. (Corn is corn and hog bellies are hog bellies.) Your prospect may aproach it this way: Is your "product" cheaper? No. Is it currently available from the incumbent? Yes. Is delivery satisfactory? Probably.

The only way you can overcome the incumbent relationship, with price and delivery being the same, is with the skills of an attacker. However, you don't want to "play" here because *this is a product-driven market* which forces you to be a "tell" seller: "let me tell you what I've got; let me tell you why it's good for you." Contrast that with: "let me find out who you are, what you need, what drives you, and let me fill those needs."

All Things Being Approximately Equal....

The next step up the ladder of appeal is the point at which product or service "A" is *approximately* equal to product or service "B". A key characteristic of this step is that the consumer has to give up something in order to get something; a concession of some kind has to be made. For example, your prospects receive some advantage from you that they don't with another professional, and you receive some advantage from them, as well. *This is a feature-driven market.*

If the consumer is weighing both "A" and "B"

and comes to the conclusion that there are some differences in features but that they are equal in terms of value to him or her, what criteria does he use to make his decision? He ultimately comes back to **price and delivery.**

Here is what is going on in your prospect's or client's mind: "Yes, they're a *little* different.... but is one cheaper than the other? Is one available, not available? Do I have a relationship in place with either of these two?" If you don't "win" on price and delivery, you will probably lose in the feature-driven strategy. In other words, to the prospect a professional services provider is a professional services provider and there is not *enough* difference in features to overcome incumbency.

All Things Are Not Equal . . . .

At the next step in the marketing ladder of appeal, product or service "A" is clearly, identifiably superior to product or service "B." To use an automobile illustration it's a Mercedes versus a Chevrolet. If someone asked your prospect whether he wanted a Mercedes or a Chevrolet for $10,000, which one do you think he would he pick? *This is a quality-driven market and its chief buying characteristic is that it requires individual judgment.*

Here's a judgment scenario: if a Mercedes is $20,000 and a Chevrolet $10,000, which one would *you* buy? *Leaning towards the Mercedes*? Now, the real prices: a Mercedes at $60,000 or a Chevrolet at $10,000; now which one would you buy? *Leaning towards the Chevrolet*? "Yes," you say, "the Mercedes is a superior piece of equipment, but it is not worth the $50,000 difference; I can do other things with that money."

I would suggest to you that to operate in the quality-driven market, to subject yourself to the individual judgment of your prospects and clients, is not where you want to be.

Here is where you want to be.

You Stand Alone

At this level, it is just "A" — *there is no choice.* You are the only candidate, the only answer in the marketplace for what the prospect or client needs or wants. At the beginning of this chapter, we concluded that a market could indeed be one individual buyer. Is it then possible for just one person to come to believe that *you* are the only alternative for his or her professional services? YES — and your next task as a marketer of yourself is *to see how many times you can duplicate that vision of you in the marketplace.* Remember, you don't need "everyone" to come to that belief; you need only a small, valued group who will give you all of their business.

In order for your clients and prospects to hold this belief about you, you have to bring to them something of unique, added value, something proprietary, something so special that it separates you from all others. It is YOU — *you are the only one who has you to market.*

There are four steps required to make yourself unsurpassably unique in the marketplace — **research, position, access,** and **control.** You don't need any of these if you wish to continue working with the low asset base market — that is, marketing and selling to consumers at the lower levels of the economic spectrum. But if you intend to aim higher, to go for the upscale consumer, you must **research** who they are, what they buy, and why; you must **position yourself** based on the research you've done to be the only viable alternative for fulfilling their needs; you must devise **campaigns to have access** to them in the appropriate style, location, and time; and, finally, you must **control your position** in your marketplace for long-term success.

The second half of this book is devoted to implementing these four steps and helping you put into practice the ideas discussed so far. But first, who is this elusive "upscale consumer" — and what makes this person "tick"?

You Can't Cold-Call the Forbes 400

Obviously you can't — and the Forbes 400, while it certainly contains the creme de la creme of the upscale market, is not the only place you'll find prospects and clients with sizeable assets.

One morning earlier in my career I met a fellow who had on a pair of Brogan shoes, khaki britches, a rather sad looking baseball cap, and a blue shirt with "Carrier" on the back. He also had a big chew of Redman Tobacco in the corner of his mouth and looked like he hadn't shaved in a couple of days.

Is this guy a prospect? He certainly doesn't look like one — he doesn't have a string of those initials like M.D., D.D.S., J.D., Ph.D., CPA strung after his name. He doesn't wear a nice starched white collar and drive a Mercedes to the country club where he chases the little white ball around. This guy just does not fit our image of a prospect.

This man owns a heating and air conditioning sales and service company, one with 127 employees and 40 trucks on the road. His company does $5 million in gross revenue a year and clears 20 percent to the bottom line, but he doesn't have those initials after his name and he doesn't look right, act right, or even smell right from time to time. *And* he drives a pickup truck to work. You wouldn't want a client that drives a truck to work, would you? The richest man in the U.S. passed away last year; Sam Walton still drove a pickup truck to work even after he was a billionaire.

Much has been written about the "affluent" investor; so much, in fact, that you'd think we would all instantly be able to pinpoint one if he or she walked in the door. Alas, that is not true, as the story above illustrates.

While their images may belie our stereotypical views, most demographers and those who have studied the affluent agree that, at least in one regard, they all share a common buying habit. According to a study of upscale consumers done by the Harvard Business School, *upscale investors buy financial services or products most often because they feel that they and their problems are understood by the seller — not because the buyer is made to understand the product by an insistent salesperson.*

The survey offered three *additional* "governing principles" for marketing and selling to the upscale consumer:

• The sales process should be built around trust-bond relationships that require openness and honesty on the part of both client and salesperson.

• People strive for the right to make their own decisions, even if they are poor decisions. They resent being manipulated and controlled, even if the solution is valid.

• If you impose solutions, they will resent both you and your solution. Pinpoint problems; but don't solve them; let the client solve them with your consultative and persuasive assistance.

This last point deserves special emphasis.
While the upscale consumer may be decisive, he
or she may resent your push to do all things for
all needs or problems at once. E. James ("Jim")
Wisner, president and chief executive officer of Financial Service Corporation, an Atlanta-based organization supporting the independent financial
service professional and a 25-year veteran of the
business, believes that where many practicing professionals err in their approach is "to do too much
for one client too fast. Your aim should be to improve a client's situation — not fix it. If you improve
it now, you'll be invited back later for more 'im-
provements'."

Jim, like many other financial services professionals, decided 25 years ago as a neophyte with
CIGNA (then Connecticut General), to aim high —
for the well-to-do business owner.

"When I started, I sort of stumbled on to some
business executives and small business owners. I
began just calling them and asking to see them —
and many agreed. I didn't know any better. After
about 18 months in business, I 'learned' that you
really shouldn't try to see business owners and
professionals in the day. Here I was, 23 years old,
and that's what I'd been doing all along. Prospects
had defenses up then; they have them up now."

CIGNA did some market research on the affluent consumer over 20 years ago that Jim believes is
"timeless" in its general segmentation of the marketplace. The largest group identified, approxi-

mately 50 percent, were those in the "too busy" category — smart, well educated professionals with good net worth but people for whom planning and managing their own investments is a time sacrifice they're not willing to make. Their focus is *earning the money.*

A smaller group, 20 percent, were "hobbyists," people with money who want to do it themselves — tracking the market on computers and buying their investments directly, through discount brokerage firms. The final 30 percent were primarily small business owners and entrepreneurs; they were "not interested" in talking with a financial service provider. CIGNA's research indicated, however, that "not interested" meant these prospects were simply hard to get to in a cold marketing manner; you must have a referral to get their business.

Although the percentages may change over time, CIGNA's 20-year-old generalizations about the interest and habits of the affluent market segment hold some truisms for the '90s. The affluent will *always* include the "hobbyists," the "too busy," and the "not interested," whether they're doctors and attorneys with significant incomes, senior business executives with a big chunk of assets building up in qualified retirement plans, owners of small closely-held businesses with most of their assets invested in their businesses, or the truly wealthy (think Rockefeller or DuPont) with control and discretion over a large, liquid asset base.

The Millionaire: Who Is This Person, Really?

Most of the country's affluent may not drive a 1970s pickup truck to work like Sam Walton or wear blue jeans and sneakers to the office like software magnate Steve Jobs. In fact, when contrasted with the wealthy, particularly "old money", in Europe and other parts of the world, America's affluent have a surprising propensity to view themselves as middle class and, in fact, even behave and consume in some pretty middle class ways. On the other hand, there are many "pseudo-affluent" individuals who behave as if they are truly affluent.

Thomas J. Stanley, Ph.D., is a former marketing professor at Georgia State University in Atlanta, Ga., and now head of the Affluent Market Institute. He has extensively studied the affluent marketplace and its consuming habits and has become quite an expert on millionaires. Over the last decade he has personally interviewed hundreds of millionaires and surveyed thousands using other statistical methods.

According to Dr. Stanley, "the average American millionaire realizes significantly less than 10 percent of his net worth in annual income. Thus, in spite of having considerable wealth and substantial increases in wealth (in unrealized form), the typical American millionaire may personally be cash poor. Often, the realized income of American millionaires is not enough to support an ostentatious consumption lifestyle." (© Dr. Thomas J. Stanley, "Marketing To The Affluent," 1988, Dow Jones-Irwin, used with permission.)

Stanley also notes that, despite the *appearance* of wealth being everywhere, the *reality* of wealth is sometimes surprising. Consider these statistics he cites in "Marketing To The Affluent":

"While neighborhood taxonomic systems will certainly identify high concentrations of wealth, most of the households that reside in the so-called prestigious neighborhoods are not in the millionaire league. In fact, many people who live in neighborhoods whose average house value is in the top 5 percent in America do not generate six-figure incomes. I estimate that in 1984 fewer than one half of the households that lived in homes valued at $300,000 or more had annual incomes of more than $100,000. A major objective of many people who live in upscale neighborhoods is to demonstrate upper-middle-class membership. Perhaps these people all completed a course in social class theory in which their instructor told them that society would rank them as upper middle class if they (1) had high-status occupational positions (corporate executives, professionals, or owners of major businesses), (2) owned a large home, (3) lived in a prestigious dwelling area, and (4) had income from inherited sources or earned sources [W. Lloyd Warner et al., Social Class in America, New York: Harper

Torch Books, 1960, p. 123].

"Proprietors of small businesses (the segment I estimate to contain the largest number of American millionaires) are ranked fifth or third from the bottom on a seven-point scale of status characteristics. On the other hand, one can be very upper middle class and have a level of net worth nowhere near seven figures and an income of less than six figures. It is my belief that the number of households in America that are interested in looking wealthy is far greater than the number that are interested in being wealthy."

Stanley further discovered in his research that wealth is frequently tied to the ownership of private or closely-held businesses. Of the millionaires in this country, 80 percent are first generation millionaires. Most of the millionaires have both a financial and managerial interest in a small or medium sized corporation, partnership, or sole proprietorship. He found that most affluent individuals own one or more businesses, but that most business owners are not affluent.

"Examine the factors that account for the wealth accumulation of a typical American millionaire. He owns or owned a business that generated annual receipts of between $500,000 and $5 million. (This revenue range accounts for more than four out of five self-made business owner millionaires.) His business is or was likely to be in the top 10 percent of all firms in its industry in terms of profitability. Yes, wealth accumulation depends on much more than the business owner's choice of industry. How he operates his business, his consumption lifestyle, his propensity to invest, how long he has been in the business, luck, and many other factors are significant." ("Marketing To The Affluent," used with permission.)

The Era Of The 'Influents'

At the beginning of the '90s, marketers, demographers, marketing consultants, and unofficial lifestyle chroniclers rushed to put the proper spin on the new decade dawning. For whatever reason or reasons, societal demographics and psychographics do seem to shift, sometimes subtly, at the change of a decade, with each 10-year span nurturing its own distinctive rhythm, priorities, attitudes, and value "realignments," providing some break with the past.

Town and Country, the ultimate affluent lifestyle magazine and one intimately familiar with discerning markets if ever there was one, published a report in 1990 on what it calls "The Era of the Influents." For this research, they commissioned the distinguished futurist Laurel Cutler, a former vice president-consumer affairs for Chrysler and a partner in FCB/Leber Katz Partners, a New York

marketing agency. The Town and Country research offers some salient points *and* challenges
for marketers of both products and services in the
'90s.

As America continues to shed the last vestiges
of the "rich and famous, conspicuous consumption"
lifestyle of the '80s, the more affluent consumer,
the leading edge of a maturing population, has em-
braced new values and attitudes, among them: *a re-
newed interest in tradition*, a shift *from the "Me Generation" to the "We Generation"*, a *search for value*
in products, services, and relationships, and *a real
concern for the future*, along with an awareness that
the future will not just take care of itself. Cutler
points out that more affluent households (defined
as those with incomes over $75,000, and one could
argue with that as being affluent) are growing at a
rate faster than any other. By 1994, the affluent
category will represent over 15 percent of all U.S.
households, compared to just 1.5 percent in 1980.

This new economic and community leadership
group was labeled the "Influents" — a hybrid demographic cluster combining *affluence* with *influence*
and merging the "values and reasoned conservatism
of both entrepreneurial and established wealth."
The Influents are keenly concerned with high standards and the integrity of a good name and have
forced a changed climate for marketers — a move
away from "mass" to "class."

Among the challenges for marketers in the '90s
is one that is crucial for professionals marketing

themselves and their services: *to build a reputation for personal service in recognition of the affluent market's segmented nature and its expectation of higher performance and standards.* The Influents are disinclined to settle for second-rate products and services and those with fleeting advantage.

These are the consumers that can put you at the top of the ladder of personal appeal where *you* and all you represent are the *only* alternative to what this discriminating investor wants and needs.

The Influents — entrepreneur millionaires and the "old money" group — may indeed continue to lead us through the '90s, but their values, attitudes, and consuming and investing habits didn't just materialize at the stroke of midnight on December 31, 1989. For a fuller understanding of their "roots", you must return to the past. It's time to begin your research.

Summary — Chapter 4:

• *There are four "rungs" on the ladder of personal appeal:*
  - *where service/product A is equal to B*
  - *where service/product A is approximately equal to B*
  - *where service/product A is clearly superior to B*
  - *where service/product A is the clear and resounding choice — there is no alternative.*

• *If service/product A equals B, this is a product driven market which forces you to be a "tell" seller.*

• *If service/product A is approximately equal to B, this is a feature driven market. If there are not <u>enough</u> differences in features to overcome incumbency, you cannot be successful here.*

• *If service/product A is clearly superior to B, this is a quality driven market that requires individual judgment by your prospects or clients.*

• *If service/product A is the clear, "winning" choice, then the prospect or client has come to the belief that you are the choice they want. You are at the top of the ladder of personal appeal. Your task is to see how many times you can duplicate that belief about you in the marketplace.*

• *The four required steps to market yourself are research, position, access, and control.*

• *Upscale investors buy financial services or products most often because they feel that they and their problems are understood by the seller — not because the buyer is made to understand the product by an insistent salesperson.*

5

PERCEPTION *IS* REALITY

"Well, what are you? What is it about you that you have always known as yourself? What are you conscious of in yourself: your kidneys, your liver, your blood vessels? No. However far back you go in your memory it is always some external manifestation of yourself where you come across your identity: in the work of your hands, in your family, in other people. And now, listen carefully. You in others — this is what you are, this is what your consciousness has breathed, and lived on, and enjoyed throughout your life, your soul, your immortality — your life in others."

Boris Pasternak, "Doctor Zhivago"

5

Have you ever sold a product to a client that was a pretty good instrument for your client's financial needs and goals, basically "did okay for them", but which that client did not completely understand?

The only reason any client would buy something from you when he or she has no idea how it works is because of trust, because you did something or said something somewhere along the way that caused that person to trust you.

If your clients are typical, they are probably not totally honest with you. That doesn't mean they're dishonest or that they overtly and consciously intend to deceive you. They just forget to tell you things. It's not because they don't trust you; after all, they bought something from you that they didn't understand. The reason we don't know everything about our clients is not that they have consciously decided not to tell us, it's that *we haven't asked*. If you have a client who says to you, "I want 10,000 shares of IBM at the market price and I want it right now," what do you do? You will hang up that phone with your hand trembling and rush to get that order executed.

First of all, the type of client that can do that is one at the top of the demographic pyramid, the upscale client. Are they decisive or nondecisive? Do decisive people change their minds quickly and often? NO. Do they want to be in control? YES.

Don't turn loose of that phone. Learn more about this client, his or her spouse, business, kids, partners, hobbies. Learn, learn, learn. The data you gather on this person will be helpful in developing your personal success profile.

This is **research**, pure and simple — the first step in the four-part process of marketing. What are you willing to learn about your prospects and clients, the markets you wish to serve? More importantly, what is *necessary* for you to know about them? Only after you've done your research can you begin to build a knowledge platform from which you can move on to **positioning** — or what your prospects and clients will come to believe about you. Remember, earlier we introduced Ries and Trout's concept and definition of positioning as "not what you do to a product or a service, but what you do to the mind of the client." Research and positioning will then allow you to devise a means of **access** to your target markets in a manner consistent with their existing behavior, habits, and buying traits.

Finally, you must gain **control** — managing the

progress of the relationship from that first thought that creeps into your prospect's mind through the first piece of business and through all subsequent business. Two primary elements are necessary to gain and maintain control of the client relationship. The first of these is the size of the group — you must be working with a small, well-defined group which does not exceed 200 in number. The second is integrity — yours. What do people believe about you? Do they see you as an honest, ethical, hard-working professional or . . . something else?

Now that we have delved into why you need to adapt your skills, why you must segment the marketplace, what the ladder of personal appeal is, and some about who the upscale consumer is, it's time to turn our attention to what to do — *you're ready to begin putting together your marketing plan.* We'll begin with research.

Research, Step #1: Who Do You Want? Who Don't You Want?

In my travels around the country working with practicing professionals, many of them ask me, "Les, what market should I be in?"

My answer is always the same: "I don't have any idea. But if you go to your client profiles you will find out!"

That's where you attack first.

If you have at least 300 client accounts you are sitting on a gold mine. You see, you don't need another 300 — you just need another 25 like the top 25 you already have. You also need a few less like the bottom 25.

I want you to do a simple exercise now, something which is a critical element of researching your markets and which will help you focus your efforts on beginning your marketing campaigns. Picture the client make-up of your practice. If you're a typical stockbroker, insurance agent, or financial planner, you probably have at least 300 clients or accounts. I have a message for you that you may not like: get rid of at least 10 percent of them. Fire them . . . give them away . . . I don't care what you do with them but "lose" them.

The relationship between your client base and your income is an inverse one in which about three-quarters of your income comes from about one-quarter of your clients. Or, for simplification, the old 80-20 rule. If you agree that's the case, why are you keeping the accounts at the bottom? Remember those brokers we interviewed who said that 200 was the maximum segment size? The other thing they unanimously told us was that they had fired 10 percent of their clients if they had more than 300. (If you've got only 22, keep them all!)

Of those 300 clients on a book of business, a large percentage have probably been around a while, and some of them may be doing absolutely nothing with you in terms of either current *or* future revenue. If 30 people have produced no revenue for you in recent memory and you "lose" them, your revenue will not drop or remain static, *it will go up* — because you will have time to work with the people that do produce revenue for you. By human nature, though, we are always reluctant to get rid of any client. Why? *They might win the lottery.* You might go broke first.

To determine which clients you want to fire, start with a three-year revenue run. Examine this historical data closely and set some identifying factors on who needs to go:

• One, they shouldn't be related to anyone at the top.

• Two, they don't give you any referrals; there's no ancillary business their relationship might bring your way.

• Three, *they don't have any money*. That's pretty simple — without money they can't do business with you!

Here's your firing strategy.

•Bullet number one: put them into a *good*, long-term investment such as a mutual fund or a wrap-fee account (something which can provide you with an on-going revenue stream), let them go to sleep, and don't wake them up when you come to work in the morning.

•Bullet number two: if clients resist your new approach, give them to a rookie — let *him* gnaw on their ankles for a while! There's nothing more tenacious than a rookie who's just been handed a few active new accounts.

•Bullet number three: find out who at your competitor firms are trying to attack your best accounts or prospects and give this client the name of that person! "This professional specializes in accounts just like yours. And he is so *good*, so *specialized*, so *busy* that you can't even get him on the phone. *You have to drop by his office and see him.*" If your competitor is busy defending himself from cast-off accounts he won't have time to attack the ones you want to keep!

Moral of this little story: a garden grows better with the weeds out. Clean house.

Once you've done that, you must break your remaining clients into clusters. These people — 8, 10, 15 in different clusters — must be as homogeneous as possible. One cluster may be "widows", one may be "entrepreneur body-shop owners." It doesn't matter what they are, but they must all be as alike as possible. If you look at the revenue produced by each group over the last three years you will discover which clusters produce the most revenue for you.

These are your target markets: more business from your active clusters and more clients just like the people in the clusters.

Research, Step #2: You Think Differently From Me

If positioning, as Ries and Trout maintain, is what you *do* to the mind of the client, then you must *know* the mind of the client . . . . "and the reality that counts is what's already in the client's mind," according to Ries and Trout.

This is the ultimate challenge of positioning — determining and analyzing what is in your clients' and prospects' minds so that you will understand their system of BAVI — the **beliefs**, **attitudes**, **values**, and **information** that comprise their reality. Just as understanding positioning requires a recognition that reality *is* perception, understanding the BAVI of a prospect or client requires a recognition that it is not important whether beliefs, attitudes, values, and information of a client *are* true, but that the client *believes* them to be true and worthwhile.

Let's first briefly define each of these terms by simply consulting a dictionary.

A **belief** is "anything believed or accepted as true, an opinion, expectation, or judgment; belief implies mental acceptance of something as true, whether based on reasoning, prejudice, or the authority of the source." **Attitude** is "a manner of acting, feeling, or thinking that shows one's disposition or opinion." **Values** are "certain estimates of worth on something in a scale of values"; they are also "acts, customs, institutions, etc. regarded in a particular, especially favorable, way by a people or ethnic group." **Information** is "knowledge acquired in any manner; facts; data; learning; lore. Information applies to facts that are gathered in any way, as by reading, observation, hearsay, etc. and does not necessarily connote validity."

Taken together, beliefs, attitudes, values, and information form the *realities of the client's mind* and make up a system by which a personal profile can be fashioned.

Each individual's set of BAVI is different, because of age, gender, experience, upbringing, ethnic heritage, religious background, education — these all play a part in forming different value systems. Most of us wind up in trouble when we begin to evaluate someone else by our value system. It's not a question of right or wrong. *"Gee, you think differently from me. You must be stupid. And you're wrong."*

My wife, Linda, used to think I was dumb, misinformed, and just plain wrong about the way I like to spend my spare time. Being a good old Southern boy, I'm into football, basketball, baseball. Linda thought my Sunday afternoons watching gladiators on the astroturf was dumb. She, on the other hand, is more into ballet. I used to think she was downright *uninformed* for liking ballet!

A couple of years ago when Mikhail Baryshnikov came to Atlanta, Linda wanted badly to go see him. I wasn't the slightest bit interested. No, no, no, I said; I do not want to spend an evening watching men in tutus, or whatever they wear, jumping around a stage. I thought it was pretty dumb, but finally I decided that I should make the effort to understand her values and beliefs about ballet.

Unbeknown to her, I got two fourth-row, center section tickets to Baryshnikov. Then I went to Nei-man-Marcus and bought her a new silk dress and some *real* jewelry to go with it. I rented a stretch limousine, put two bottles of Dom Perignon on ice, went to her office at the end of the day, and said, "Get dressed. We're going to the ballet." It was a $3,500 date with a woman to whom I had been married 18 years.

You know what I discovered? Her beliefs, attitudes, and values were not *wrong* at all — the ballet was pretty interesting (though still somewhat boring) and I learned a fair amount about it. (She eventually learned to be a little "smarter" about football, too!)

No matter how hard we try we cannot "take on" the values of another person. The values of others will always vary from our own. Values are not right and wrong; values are only *different*.

The Effects of the Cohort Effect

Dr. Morris Massey, a noted psychologist and business consultant, put forth a theory some years ago that can serve us well in understanding our prospects and clients. Dr. Massey's research indicated that the value systems people have in place as adults are generally formed during the 10th year of life and, further, that 90 percent of those values will stay with a person for life.

Where were your clients at the age of 10? What were their experiences and how have they helped mold their current values? If you explore this, you will go a long way towards understanding your clients' value systems and — the ultimate goal — towards becoming the choice for fulfilling *their* needs in a manner which matches *their* values.

Let's do a few profiles on some prospects using this concept of chronological age and value formation. We'll start with me.

I was 10 years old in 1953. I was born to a reasonably comfortable lifestyle ("middle class American") in the South. I was a Boy Scout, an athlete through junior high and high school, went to church on Sunday morning, Youth Group on Sunday night.

Who was in the White House in 1953? Eisenhower — the brave general, the victor of World War II, a leader and commander, and, to me, a strong grandfather-type image. Could you trust a government led by Eisenhower? Absolutely. Could you trust the banks in 1953? Absolutely. Could you trust the big corporations in 1953? Absolutely. ("If it's good for General Motors it's good for America.") After all, many of your fathers went to work for a big company and stayed there their entire careers.

In 1953 you could trust corporations, the banks,

the government. Think about how the stock market performed in the '50s: it was the best single decade in history in terms of percentage gain. You would have had to work hard to lose money in stocks if you had held them through the '50s.

Knowing these things about me, what do you think my value system consists of? Motherhood, apple pie, the Green Bay Packers, and Chevrolet — "persona Americana." What am I likely to be an owner of? The great American corporations. Yes; I'm a typical equity buyer who believes that the only way to wealth is to own companies. I don't believe in loaning my money out — you can't *give* me a bond.

What if I had been 10 years old in 1933? That year, this country was in the grip of a terrible Depression. FDR was in the White House and he was put there on this premise: "I will look out for you. We're going to put your fathers back to work." It was the New Deal.

Could you trust the banks in 1933? No; they were going broke. Could you trust the big corporations in 1933? No; unemployment was 26 percent and corporations were laying people off right and left. Who could you trust in 1933? THE GOVERN-MENT. That is why someone 65 or 70 years old today will buy almost anything that says "government" on it. The government put their fathers back to work when there was nothing to eat.

What if I had been 10 years old in 1973? Nixon was in the White House. Could you trust a government led by Nixon? *Well* . . . . Could you trust the banks in 1973? Interest rates were 14 percent and rising, the oil embargo had its stranglehold on us, and banks were loaning money to Third World dictators — huge amounts of debt with the prospect of repayment looking pretty poor. How about big corporations? Could you trust them? In 1973, they were getting pretty good at something we're still paying for — polluting the environment. Some of our biggest corporations were putting things in the ground that have a halflife of forever.

Who, then, could you trust in 1973? NOT ANYONE OVER 30. When you talk to young people today, those in their late-20s or early 30s, what do they want? They want BMWs and carphones and sailing trips around the Greek Isles — *and they want them now.* What, me worry? They want it now because when they were 10 years old the world was going to hell in a handbasket and that's when their values were formed.

When you think about these examples, many of your clients will probably come to mind. There are always exceptions, but by and large the phenomenon called the Cohort Effect applies. The Cohort Effect holds that people who grew up in the same period, or generation, experience many of the same things that color and shape their viewpoints the rest of their lives. The effect is particularly strong for members of the Depression-era generation. Baby-boomers, the largest and most influential generation and demographic group in history, reflect a dual Cohort Effect — early boomers may have been heavily influenced by the Civil Rights movement; later ones by Watergate and Vietnam.

BAVI is a powerful concept that is critical in understanding your clients and, subsequently, in positioning yourself for their needs. Using the principles of BAVI, let's profile to "position" with a hypothetical client.

You're Not In the Mind Changing Business

Your prospect is 72 years old, has $400,000 in assets, his home is paid for, and his only other source of income is Social Security. What does this client want, above all else? SAFETY. What does he have to have? INCOME. (Wanting and needing, as we all know, are two   different things.) The key question this prospect has to grapple with is: how much safety do I have to give away to get the income I must have to survive? That's a negotiation process.

In your conversations with this prospect, let's suppose that he says to you: "Gee, I think Alpha-Beta Advisory is the best investment house in the world." (*You* work for AlphaBeta's biggest competitor!) Uh-oh; what are you going to do with this piece of BAVI that's just been dropped on you? You have four choices.

The first is capitulation; pack it in and leave.

"You're right. Goodbye." Well, that certainly
doesn't serve the needs either *one* of you have — his
for safety and income, yours for a client.
The second alternative is to be defensive.
"You've got to be kidding! Those guys at Alpha-
Beta are thieves and crooks; they don't know what
they're doing!" You *won't* win this fight. The third
alternative is "Oh *yeah*? Why exactly do you think
so?" You're likely to get multiple reasons why this
client thinks so, and now you have *several* obstacles
to overcome! That doesn't work so well, either.

Do you really care whether this client thinks
AlphaBeta Advisory is the best investment house in
the world? It doesn't matter. *It doesn't affect whether
you can provide this client with safety and income.* You
are not in the mind-changing business, and the
chances are slight that you're going to change his
mind anyway. It's like a judge telling a jury to
"kindly disregard those remarks."

What you really want to do is to be able to position yourself uniquely with what's already in his
mind — even *align* yourself with it. The natural tendency is to say: "You know, you're right. AlphaBeta's
done a great job for clients for years, *BUT. . . . ."*
That is a big mistake. When you use that word,
you are disagreeing with what you've just said;
you are contradicting yourself. When you do that
to the *client* you are saying that his beliefs, attitudes, values, and information are *wrong*. Dismiss
this word from your vocabulary because your
prospects or clients will not, and should not, tol-

erate it when you say to them: "The beliefs you hold sacred and dear are incorrect."

Try this approach instead. "AlphaBeta's done a great job for clients for years. *I* provide opportunities that can render high retirement income in a predictable fashion."

This approach is simple, powerful, and it leaves your client's values intact and *positions you to do for them what they want to have happen.* This prospect wants a predictable income stream. Your competitor firm may just *be* the most powerful investment house in the world, but what does that have to do with you providing what this prospect wants?

"I provide predictable income streams." You are defining yourself in terms of what the prospect wants to have happen — that is your position.

Summary — Chapter 5 :

• *The first step in research is "cleaning up" your current book of business. Fire some clients — you can't necessarily afford to keep them all, especially if they produce no income for you.*

• *When you break your remaining clients into clusters, you will discover your true target markets: more business from your active clusters and more clients like those in the clusters.*

• *The ultimate challenge of positioning is understanding your clients' beliefs, attitudes, values, and information. This is their reality.*

• *Psychologists tell us that the value systems people have in place as adults are generally formed during the 10th year of life. Know thy client!*

• *Don't fight your clients' set of BAVI. Instead, position yourself to achieve their objectives while leaving their values intact.*

6

NO WIMPS ALLOWED

"Words are things, and a small drop of ink, falling like dew upon a thought, produces that which makes thousands, perhaps millions, think."

Lord Byron

6

Your position is your niche inside the reality of the client's mind. To get to this crucial, second point in the four-step marketing process requires, first, that you've done your research, as discussed in Chapter 5. It also requires developing strong positioning statements — the necessary tools for establishing your own *unique* position of appeal to your target markets.

According to Max Carey, the president of Corporate Resource Development and a colleague of mine when I was employed there, "a good positioning statement will allow you to make the transition from product- or technical-driven selling to client- and competitor-driven marketing. It is the critical step in the differentiation process because it facilitates movement in the relationship." *It is how you make you unique.*

There are certain "rules" that have evolved over the years for what a positioning statement must do:

• It must **be of value in the eyes of the customer**

or prospect. This is "I provide income streams" vs. "I sell mutual funds."

• It must **define briefly what the company, product, or individual does in relation to the competition** and **differentiate you or your products from the competition.** A good example is your response to our prospect in Chapter 5 who has "positive BAVI" about AlphaBeta: "You are absolutely right. AlphaBeta's done a great job for clients for years. I have the systems that can maximize retirement income in a predictable fashion."

• It must **establish brand versus generic positioning.** That brand is you.

• It must be **believable yet intriguing.** It must stimulate the client in some fashion so that it causes him or her to ask, "How do you do that?" The objective is to open up the mind.

• It is very important that a positioning statement use **strong action words.** "I specialize in assisting clients" doesn't specifize *anything* for *anybody,* not you, not the client. Throw out the word specialize; it's wimpy and overworked. Use action verbs — maximize, minimize, build, provide, reduce, enhance, protect.

• Finally, it must be **easily understood** by the client or prospect. No jargon.

In "Power Marketing: The 101 Best Strategies for Financial Professionals," authors Richard Wollack and Alan Parisse offer an interesting, even humorous, look at the tendency that financial professionals have to get caught up in the jargon of the profession, using buzzwords that may not make a lot of sense to clients. Wollack and Parisse suggest using The Investment Buzzword Generator as an example of industry jargon, words that are not only misunderstood but frequently misused, to determine whether you are guilty of jargon-speak with your clients. "The Investment Buzzword Generator," say Wollack and Parisse, "takes independently legitimate financial terms and combines them to create nonsensical phrases that often have an authentic sound."

Rules for playing the game: select three random numbers from each column of buzzwords on the next page to generate a phrase. Some of them sound remarkably similar to jargon we may use with our clients. (Used with permission: "Power Marketing," by Richard Wollack and Alan Parisse, © 1991 by Dearborn Financial Publishing, Inc., Published by Dearborn Financial Publishing, Inc./Chicago. All rights reserved.)

The Investment Buzzword Generator

1. Adjusted	1. Depreciable	1. Accruals
2. Staged	2. Wraparound	2. Assets
3. Reportable	3. Crossover	3. Expenses
4. Sheltered	4. Managed	4. Risks
5. Tangible	5. Intangible	5. Write-offs
6. Leveraged	6. Recovery	6. Gains
7. Mortgaged	7. Underwriting	7. Notes
8. Allowable	8. Promissory	8. Liability
9. Deductible	9. Public	9. Costs
10. Legal	10. Deferred	10. Debt
11. Taxable	11. Development	11. Equity
12. Convertible	12. Capitalization	12. Capital
13. Improved	13. Acquisition	13. Losses
14. Leased	14. Unrealized	14. Proceeds
15. Registered	15. Liquidating	15. Dividends
16. Exempt	16. Preference	16. Cashflow
17. Discounted	17. Reinvestment	17. Bonds
18. Earned	18. Economic	18. Annuities
19. Passive	19. Portfolio	19. Distributions
20. Active	20. Private	20. Bonus

Have you ever talked to your client about "tangible reinvestment costs" or "discounted economic accruals" or "staged promissory dividends"? Would your client consider these his or her investment objectives? I think you get the idea what avoiding jargon is all about.

Now, here are some "rules" for what positioning statements should *not* be:

• **NOT created from the salesperson's point-of-view**. Why not? *Because it isn't your money*, to put it bluntly. They don't care what your point of view is; they're only concerned with *their* point of view.   In your prospect's mind is "maximize income in a predictable fashion." For you, that may mean a bond fund or a direct investment with an eight or nine percent cash flow on it and a tax advantage. But that's what you want to sell, not what he wants to buy. He wants a predictable income stream.

• **NOT overly complicated or too technical**. If you say to the client, "Gosh, you'll really like the Omnipotent Fund. It's got a Beta of .80", he may look back at you and say, *"Beta? I thought Beta went out when VHS came in . . . ."* It doesn't mean anything to him.

On the other hand, if you say, "You'll like Omnipotent Fund. It's a good, dependable fund that buys big Blue Chip stocks that weather down markets well", and he says, "Oh, how does it do that?", then you are justified in using some technical information or data in support of your statement.

Use technical explanations *only* to validate or bridge.

• **NOT too wordy.** One brief sentence will do. A positioning statement is not intended to be a thesis.

Let me give you an example of what I believe is the most powerful positioning statement in the financial services industry, the most powerful four words ever used as a company tagline: "ROCK SOLID. MARKET WISE." What is it clients want to hear when they're evaluating someone to handle their hard-earned money? They want someone strong, capable, SOLID. And, regardless of what the market is doing, they want someone WISE about it. These four words are extremely customer-driven.

• **NOT full of unbelievable superlatives.** This is the "all things to all people under all circumstances at all times" approach. Government funds are not paying 12 or 14 percent, not now and not in the mid '80s when clients were told that. "You want 13 percent? Well, that's what it pays." The only problem was that clients found out later that particular product, by itself, really didn't "pay" that. We just kind of hedged them up there. Then the hedges got trimmed and so did the clients, as the bonds were called away.

• **NOT set in an adversarial tone.** Don't forget every individual's BAVI.

• **NOT WIMPY.** This bears repeating. Trying to gain a prospect as a client is not the time to be wimpy; it's the time to stand up and be heard. *Use action verbs.* Successful marketing means declaring a strong, solid, dependable position in the client's mind that differentiates you and provides some action-oriented advantage to the client.

In formulating your positioning statement, you have to position three critical elements: the person (you), the product, and the company. Do not put them in the same positioning statement. *You* come first, because *if they don't buy you they don't really care what your company has to offer.* Your company, through name and reputation, may embellish your position, but you have to sell yourself first.

Take a look at the sample personal positioning statements that follow. Steal them; modify them; come up with your own that are similar, and *use them* as you position yourself in certain markets.

Retirement Income:

• I provide the instruments that can result in predictable income streams from the asset bases of retired oil company executives. (MAKE IT AS SPECIFIC AS YOU CAN AS OFTEN AS YOU CAN!)

• I build dependable, predictable income for retired small business owners who must depend on the income stream from a lifetime of asset accumulation.

• I help protect assets from inflation and taxation while providing predictable income streams.

Pre-Retirement Wealth Building:

• I identify and secure the opportunities that can build the wealth of entertainment industry executives.

• I implement investment strategies that can provide for lifestyle continuation after retirement.

• I execute the investment strategies professional athletes need to build a secure asset base from high, short-term incomes.

Young Professionals:

• I bring professional and timely execution of investment planning to college professors, which can build an early asset base.

• I guard and treat the financial health of medical professionals.

Tax Planning Needs:

• I provide tax-free growth of asset bases for self-employed commercial artists.

• I implement tax-free investment strategies for Pennsylvania professionals — no Federal, no State, no personal property taxes.

Clarity in identification is critical.

In "Bottom Up Marketing," Al Ries and Jack Trout

urge marketing chieftains to "go down to the front" in order to get a real handle on the marketplace and the customers that comprise it. They offer these comments on the "specificity" that today's consumers are seeking:

"Take the boom in financial services companies. Everybody is selling, promoting, and marketing financial services.

"Stockbrokers don't sell stocks anymore. They sell financial services: annuities, mutual funds, municipal bonds. Life insurance companies don't just sell you life and property insurance anymore. To quote from a Travelers ad, they sell 'diversified financial services' including mortgage financing, retirement programs, mutual funds, HMOs, and PPOs.

"Commercial banks want to be your financial partner for life, with credit cards, insurance, you name it..... Go down to the front lines of the financial services war and listen to customers and prospects. Did you ever hear a customer use the words 'financial services'? As in, 'Let's go down to the Savings and Loan, dear, and get some financial services'.

"Customers don't generalize; they *specifize*. They talk in terms of mortgages, stocks, car insurance, annuities, home equity loans. Yet companies trying to sell these customers are doing just the opposite. They promote themselves as suppliers of a full range of financial services. In the military analogy we call this 'attacking on a wide front.' And it almost never works."

Consumers do specifize about products but, more than that, they seek *solutions* to specific needs and that is why a strong, powerful positioning statement is so critical. The stock, the annuity, or the retirement plan may *be* the answer to their problem but what they ultimately want is what your offering it provides to them — "I implement investment strategies that can provide for lifestyle continuation after retirement." That is the specificity they want.

The Power to Influence

The words you use in your positioning statements for your various markets are, as you can see, powerful — "the most powerful drug used by mankind," as Rudyard Kipling said of words. They have the power to influence your prospects and clients in provocative, meaningful ways.

In the book "The Seven Secrets of Influence" (an excellent book that I suggest you read), author and management consultant Elaina Zuker offers, as her first six "secrets", six different styles of influence predicated on language and method of delivery. (The seventh secret is optimizing your influence by using one of your six styles.)

Summarized below are Zucker's six styles — the secrets of influence. (Elaina Zuker, "The Seven Secrets of Influence," © 1991, McGraw-Hill, Inc., used with permission.)

- **The Telling/Analyst Style**:
  People who use this style are direct in presenting their ideas, which they support with evidence and arguments. This person prefers logic to emotion, justifies arguments or ideas with reasons and evidence, values structure and organization, likes to integrate and link into others' points, and is inclined to elaborate on positions. Telling is the style of the analyst.
  If *you* are a teller in style, you are likely to say things like: "Let me *tell* you . . . . " or "The *data demonstrate* . . . ."
  If *your prospect or client* is a teller/analyst, he or she might like statistics or data in order to evaluate your recommendations; these people care a lot about substance.

- **The Compelling/Pragmatist Style**:
  The person with the compelling style (a typical example would be a schoolteacher, a sports coach, or "The One Minute Manager") lets others know up front what he or she wants, expects, or requires of others and is in a position to judge compliance or performance and administer approval, disapproval, reward, and punishment. The compelling

style is most effective when the other person's level of motivation or need for the "reward" (approval, acceptance, respect, etc.) that you control is high. The compeller is practical, pragmatic, and results-oriented.

If *you* are a compeller/pragmatist, you are likely to speak this way: "We *expect* to *achieve* . . . . "

If *your client or prospect* is a compeller/pragmatist, he or she wants to know what "rewards" are in store, as well as the negative consequences. A compeller welcomes negotiation and bargaining as part of the influence process — if something is presented to them in *absolute* terms it doesn't seem very intriguing or exciting. Compellers also dislike "emotional" talk.

• The Felling/Preservationist Style:

A good example of a feller is a bureaucrat — someone who does it the "tried and true way", who sticks to a position and attempts to gain influence or power by remaining firm, or an attorney who carefully cross-examines a witness and extracts only the information that is helpful to the case. Fellers tend to "fell" (cut down) the ideas of others. Like telling, this style uses logic and reason to influence; unlike telling, however, the feller's main focus is *reactive*, using logic to counter others' ideas. The disadvantages of the felling style are a lack of flexibility and difficulty in picking up the subtle cues in a situation.

If *you* are a feller in style of influence, you probably use this type of approach: "We can't *afford* to *experiment . . . . "*

If *your client or prospect* is a feller/preservationist, don't meander on with long, rambling, small talk. Joining with fellers by assisting them in doing what they want to do gives them the feeling that you understand where they are coming from. Be attentive and flexible.

- **The Welling/Catalyst Style**:

This is the "heart to heart" style, the ability to easily gain rapport with others. The welling/catalyst style is flexible, actively encourages others' suggestions, listens to both verbal and non-verbal cues, rephrases when necessary, and elaborates. The weller's objective of establishing rapport, a relationship based on mutual trust and shared feelings, is accomplished by disclosing one's feelings, being loyal, keeping confidences, and supporting others' ideas and feelings.

If *you* are a weller/catalyst, you may use a phrase like this: "We need to *mutually agree upon . . . . "*

If *your client or prospect* is a weller/catalyst, you should recognize that this person highly values relationships and may welcome a human interest story from you because it furthers the personal bonds that wellers consider basic to business transactions. Wellers like to listen and *they* like good listeners and give them valuable air-time. When you are presenting something to a weller, the "bare bones" approach with just the facts will not be enough.

• **The Selling/Strategist Style**:
This is the sales "artist" style, one that must be both artful and hopeful to work well. Those who are effective sellers ask probing questions early in the influence process, tailor their words and tones to the other person's, present ideas in terms of benefits to others' specific needs, and acknowledge objections.

If *you* are a seller/strategist, you probably use language like this: "Your *goals* can surely be *achieved* . . . . "

If *your client or prospect* is a seller/strategist, he or she will respond to this style if you present your recommendations in a way that addresses this basic question: "What will this product or service do for me?" A seller/strategist will respond to your attempts to gain insight into his or her decision-making process, and will even be responsive to your persistent attempts to overcome objections and get a commitment.

• **The Gelling/Idealist Style**:
When two or more people's ideas come together to form a single vibrant entity, the gelling style of influence is in action. People who use the gelling style mobilize the energy and resources of others by appealing to their hopes, values, and aspirations. Gelling requires the ability to present ideas powerfully. Its appeal is not so much to the intellect as it is to the emotions and values of others involved; this is emotion *over* logic. The geller/idealist promotes a

common vision and paints a picture of a brighter future.

If *you* are a geller/idealist in style, you probably use language like this: "My *vision* of this . . . . "

If *your client or prospect* is a geller/idealist, he will respond to your attempts to strike a common chord and to make *his* goals *your* goals. While gelling is a powerful style of influence, it is not always well-received in the business environment, where rationale and logic are the prevalent modes of communication. You may, however, find a geller/idealist in entrepreneurial settings, where "vision" is a driving force.

Zuker says that the six styles of influence can be "clustered", with overlapping characteristics common to the clusters:

• **Telling, Compelling, and Felling** form a cluster. All are logical, rational, and structured. Behaviors are proactive, controlling, and direct in their attempt to influence.

• **Welling, Selling, and Gelling** form another cluster. All are flexible, emotional, receptive, and less controlling. Good listening skills are also found in each of these styles.

• **Compelling and Selling** form a third cluster. Compelling uses rewards (negotiation and bargaining) as a means to influence; gelling offers benefits. The difference in these two styles, however, is that compellers tell what the "rewards" are, while sellers gather information on needs and try to match the reward with the need.

Zucker also offers an interesting note on the six styles: Telling, Compelling, and Felling are often viewed as stereotypically *masculine* behaviors, while Welling, Selling, and Gelling are stereotypically *feminine* behaviors.

Each style of influencing behavior can be useful and effective in certain situations with certain people, and an honest examination at the gut-check level will help you better understand your own innate style and how you may be using it, for better or for worse, with your clients and prospects. But *your* predominant style, and that of your individual clients, is only part of positioning as an element of your overall marketing campaigns.

Let's briefly review the marketing steps we've discussed so far — research and positioning — and look towards the final two — access and control.

To begin your research, you must **go to your book of business and examine it** rationally to determine what markets you are serving successfully. Part of that process will include, for many of you, firing some clients.

Then, you must **segment and identify your clients into specific clusters** by demographics and/or geographics. Demographics is any method you would use to "describe" a person — blue collar, white collar, retired, corporate executive, male, female, age, and so forth — but it must be so specific that it only describes 200 people. That group then becomes a target market; in other words, *more* clients like these that make up personal success profiles for you.

This exercise, combined with an **exploration of your clients' and prospects' beliefs, attitudes, values, and information** system will help you **build profiles** of these people. What do you know about this market? What do they want to have happen? What is of most importance to them? What secondary needs exist or are likely to arise later? These steps will then enable you to **build powerful positioning statements** for you, your products, and your company.

Fourth, all of the above is a waste of time unless you **devise a means of access to reach your target markets.** Now, you are ready to turn prospects into clients.

Summary — Chapter 6:

• *A good positioning statement will allow you to make the transition from product driven selling to client and competitor driven selling. It is how you make you unique.*

• *Positioning statements must: present value in the eyes of the customer, define briefly what the company, product, and individual does in relation to the competition, establish brand positioning, be believable yet intriguing, be easily understood, and use strong action verbs.*

• *Today's consumers are seeking specificity — specific solutions to real needs.*

• *You must be cognizant of your own language — your personal "style of influence" — and that of your clients in order to be most effective in marketing yourself.*

7

WARMING UP THE MARKET

"A salesman need never be ashamed of his calling. He should only be ashamed of his not calling."

Anonymous

7

Turning prospects into clients means devising a means of access to each of your target groups that is appropriate in style and approach. What works best for one group may not work as well — or at all — with another. You must learn to match your goals with the goals of your prospects *and* with the techniques of the various campaigns that are typically used by financial service professionals. For each type campaign that you consider implementing ask yourself: Where is my time best spent? With which campaign will I realize the greatest multiplier effect? Which has the most powerful impact?

As you reflect upon beginning new self-marketing campaigns, a good exercise is to develop a marketing worksheet that answers some questions related to each component of a successful campaign, as outlined below:

• **Define your goals or objectives in writing.**
   - How much revenue do I want to generate?

- How many new accounts do I want?
- What new markets do I want to penetrate?
• **Define the time frame.**
  - When do I begin?
  - When do I stop?
• **Identify the target market(s).**
  - How would I describe the people in this market?
  - How large is it? How many of them can I reach?
  - What kind of manageable mailing list can I develop?
• **Select the appropriate access method.**
  - Where can I find the individuals in this market?
  - What are the leisure, social, cultural, professional, and civic activities they enjoy and are likely to be involved in?
• **Build positive, powerful position statements.**
• **Identify what, if any, support is needed.**
  - What support do I need and can count on from product sponsors?
  - What support do I need and can count on from my company — people and dollars?
• **Keep score!**

After you've done your homework by reflecting on the above steps in the planning process, you can begin fashioning the appropriate means of access, one of the five types of self-marketing campaigns: **proactive/reactive, networking, captive seminars, invitation seminars,** and **referrals.** In this and the next chapter, we're going to give you a specific example of each. Let's begin with cold calling and business canvassing, one type of proactive/reactive campaign.

"Wait," you're saying, "in an earlier chapter you shot a lot of holes in cold calling." Yes, and it should be fairly obvious that the campaign with the least impact on the affluent consumer is cold calling and business canvassing, but sometimes it does work.

There is a firm in the financial service industry that has a somewhat unique policy for rookie stockbrokers. The first 30 days they are on board they are not allowed to come into the office at all. Instead, they must go out and meet business people face to face, shake hands with them, exchange cards with them. They are not allowed to sell anything *to* or do anything *for* these contacts; they just have to get out and find them and meet them. At the end of that period, they are expected to come back with five to seven business cards for each day — that translates to about 125 to 150 business leads. If, as many people maintain, marketing is still a "numbers game", these rookies are at least getting the numbers. It's an interesting technique.

Cold calling is basically a **proactive** marketing technique: pick up the phone and call someone, get out and about and press the flesh like a politician. **Reactive marketing** is when you do something that tickles the market in some fashion, it reacts, and you then respond to the reaction.

Neither proactive activities, like cold calling, or reactive activities are particularly effective by themselves, but when combined they can be very powerful. The elements of a combination power campaign include: **define the target group, develop the reactive instrument, implement proactively** (write, call, advertise, etc.) and **follow up, reposition for additional business,** and get **referrals** where appropriate.

Here are two examples of a combination proactive-reactive marketing campaign that are a little warmer than just cold calling.

The 49 Cent - 4 Hypo Campaign

Many of you in the financial service industry use "hypotheticals" fairly frequently in presenting investment alternatives to clients. If you haven't or don't, you should. Hypotheticals clearly illustrate a "real" investment to a client and can be powerful in their simplicity. Now, I'm going to tell you how you can use a hypothetical and *double its impact*. It's the 49 cent-four hypothetical campaign.

First, I'm going to define a target group — it's 50-year-old corporate executives — defined by demographics and geographics so as not to exceed 200. Generally, the primary concern of this person is planning and preparation for retirement and for income needs after retirement. Of course, the optimum age for retirement without any tax ramifications is presently 59 and 1/2, so we're going to run a 10-year hypothetical since our prospect is approximately 50 years old. Let's use an initial investment of $50,000 and apply the actual historical performance of a good mutual fund (whichever fund you choose), which of course will vary from the market's actual performance. If you use a "blue chip" equity mutual fund, the fund must have a track record of at least 25 years. (If you're calling on 50 year old executives and they don't have $50,000 to invest you're in the wrong market.) Then you must have have an "add-on" feature which increases the investment amount by $500 monthly.

Hypothetical number one, which begins 25 years in the past and runs for 10 years, is the accumulation phase, which generates a dollar value at the end of the time frame, when the prospect is approximately 60 years old. This hypothetical is followed by three separate sequential five-year hypotheticals, which we will use as the base to provide an income stream.

Hypothetical number two uses the total value from the first 10 years and then begins with an eight percent monthly systematic withdrawal from the accumulated value. (How many places could this client regularly get eight percent today? Be sure to point that fact out.) This eight percent income is paid out every month for the next five years, at which time a recalculation will produce a new value, generally an increase. We will take that new value, recalculate the eight percent, and start the payout process again for the next five years. At the end of that five year period, it will happen again.

Your client is now 75 years old and he has a significant accumulation left and has received eight percent, or more, in income over the 15-year period. And, generally speaking, he will have a *larger* asset base than with which he started.

If you show a hypothetical like this to your prospect will he reach for his checkbook?

Now, here's how to use this powerful information when the prospect is unavailable for a face-to-face meeting. Send the complete set of hypotheticals with a personal note that says: *"Please retain the enclosed information and highlighter as you will need it when I call you on Thursday. This information could be crucial to your financial future."*

The 49 cents is for a yellow highlighter. (Some mutual fund companies will even provide highlighters!) Oh, by the way — get one with a highlighter on one end and a pen on the other. *Your client will need it to write the check.*

Put the four sheets, the note, and the 49 cent highlighter in a plain white envelope with a handwritten address. Lick your own stamp and stick it on; do not send it through your company's postage machine.

A few years ago I suggested this campaign to a broker in Houston, TX. On Monday he sent out five. On Thursday he called them all. His average closing ratio was two of the five and the average ticket size was $88,000. He does this regularly now, for four weeks at a time, and then he "lays off" for a month. Why? He has *additional business to write.* He does approximately $900,000 a year in gross commission income.

It works. And it's inexpensive.

Babies Don't Have Any Money...Right?

Another "warmer" proactive-reactive campaign is with newborn babies. "Wait a minute, Les," you're saying, "babies don't have any money; they don't even have any clothes!" True. Your ultimate objective is not the baby or Mom and Dad, because they are likely to be in the entry level asset base market. Your real target is Grandma and Grandad because they typically have a higher asset base to work with.

What do all parents and grandparents have in common? They'd like this beautiful new baby to go to college — that's your quick "profile." Now you want to have your reactive piece, something that will tickle this target market, so you develop a little mailer that shows that if someone puts aside $10,000 for this little bundle of joy that money should grow significantly over the next 17 or 18 years, depending on the type of investment. (If you use an actual investment with a 20-year performance history, you will have a more powerful illustration.)

You should mail this little tickler with a "Congratulations" card only a couple of days after the birth of the child. Where do you find the babies? Births are a matter of public record—they can be found at the county courthouse or in local newspapers. In addition, some direct-mail companies offer lists of newborns. And you want to send it *to the baby* — not the parents. The baby's first piece of personal mail should be from *you!*

A couple of days after you mail it, pick up the phone and call. Keep this call short; after all, Mom and Dad are very tired and confused. Briefly introduce yourself and ask, "Have you begun to think about preparing for Sweetie Pie's college education?" The sleep-deprived new Dad says, "Who is this? I haven't even gotten the hospital bill paid!" You then position yourself by saying, "My name is Bob Smith. I can help provide the strategies for tomorrow's expensive education with cheap dollars today." Position, position, position.

Pause. "How do you do that?" Make your appointment and get armed with all manner of research and information about future college costs. Guess who's in town for the birth of the child? Grandma and Grandad. The idea is to make your presentation while they are there in the house, so you get a $2,000 commitment from one Grandad, the same from the other, and eke out $1,000 from the new parents. You now have $5,000 to start with and ask for an additional $200-300 a month to keep it going.

Now, you want to *reposition* yourself, so show your information to the parents and say, "Wouldn't it be great if we could send Sweetie Pie through college and still have something in the account to give her as a graduation gift?"

"Ooooooh, that would be wonderful. I wish somebody had done that for *me!*" Now go to your hypotheticals. You want to show them one that illustrates a 10 or 12 percent systematic withdrawal from the funds that have built up over time. This withdrawal rate, augmented by contributions from parents and the student's earnings, should take care of college, while leaving the asset base mostly intact. In a subliminal fashion, what did you just present to the subconscious mind of Grandad? *A retirement funding vehicle.*

"You mean I can put my money into this, draw out about 8 to 10 percent annually over a 10 to 20 year period, and still come away with as much or more money than I began with?" Perhaps.

So you get a large account with this Grandad, the same with the other set of grandparents — and you can still work on the new parents' retirement plan, using the same hypotheticals. And that one Congratulations card. Since it's likely that those two sets of grandparents have other children and grandchildren, those grandchildren have another set of grandparents, too. It's the financial version of the extended family.

Obviously, you may not succeed with each contact; you may only get a few a month, and by using publicly-available birth records you're going to get a wide variety from the economic and social stratum. (Hint: go for the "top dollar" private hospitals only.) This example, however, shows you how this proactive-reactive campaign can work, even with newborns.

Soaring With The Eagles

The next campaign up the marketing pyramid is **networking**. This may sound trite, because people talk about "working the network" all the time. But if you use some organization and logic you can win new clients through networking campaigns.

For our purposes, we're going to define networking two ways. The first is **establishing your own network**—an *internal* network—one that allows you to interface with people who *influence* asset holders within a targeted market. An example is the popular "lead clubs" that professionals in non-related fields form to interact with each other and share ideas and information on prospects that may need each others' services.

Think about some of the people and contacts that surround you every day, those that form an informal network and whose activities and needs can result in mutually beneficial relationships. *Your client* who is establishing a new business needs a sophisticated computerized telephone system. *You* know the top salesperson of this type equipment from your activities with your "internal" network.

Another member of your network may be an insurance agent that has a client who just received a large lump sum pension and who desperately needs investment advice. Remember Brian Lee's target market of CPAs and attorneys 200 miles from his home base?

Joan H. Peurifoy, CFP, a successful financial planner and regional director with Financial Network Investment Corporation (FNIC) in Dallas, TX, refers to the legal professionals with whom she works, usually on behalf of mutual clients, as real "centers of influence."

"When I first got into this business in 1979, you didn't have to ask for referrals from other professionals," says Joan, "they just came. About 1986 or 1987, with a lot of changes in our industry, I found it more difficult to get new clients. Now, you *have* to market yourself to other professionals. Working together on shared clients is always a challenge; we must all learn to coexist and not tread too heavily on each other."

You must respect the integrity of your internal network.

Networking within related professions is not limited to successful financial service professionals in the U.S. Paul Fyfe, National Sales Manager for Armstrong-Jones, a mutual fund management and distribution company in New Zealand with more than $3 billion under management, likes to point out that, because of the International Date Line, New Zealand and Australia are "always ahead of the

U.S." That may also be reflected by the "down under" approach to professional networking.

"In New Zealand, there is a strong movement for financial service professionals to associate themselves with an attorney or an accountant, and even for those professionals to have a financial planner actually 'housed' in their offices — a more formal partnership," says Paul. "Attorneys have seen themselves losing the client and the client's money, so they've decided they want to maintain some control. The smart and forward-thinking financial planners are saying 'you keep the attorney-client relationship and I'll just handle all the investment business'." The two share the investment fee or the financial service professional "rebates" part of the brokerage commissions. (Check with regulatory bodies as U.S. laws differ from those of other countries.)

"Professionals are really building relationships this way," says Paul. "It gives more exposure to everybody."

That's the object of the game when establishing your own network.

The second type of network marketing is **marketing through a network that is already in place,** —an *external* network—utilizing a well-developed plan to interface *directly* with major asset holders.

If I ask you where you are likely to find the wealthiest people in a metropolitan area, the first place that would likely come to mind is country clubs. Do you have access to every private club? No way. You can't just walk in and crash Daddy

Warbucks' private party can you? They're there, but they're not accessible to you. They *are*, however, accessible through cultural organizations (the arts, the ballet, the symphony, the museum guild), fund raising drives (United Way, the Humane Society, The Red Cross), the Chamber of Commerce, boards of directors of private schools and libraries, college level athletic associations, and the like.

"Les, which one should I join?" I don't know and I don't care — just get involved and work the network. For any of these groups, volunteer for the membership or fund-raising committees — they have a list of people who have money *and who give it away*!

When I returned to graduate school at Wake Forest University, I needed a job to help fund my education, so I looked around Winston-Salem and decided to go to one of the largest employers in town. I went to the Personnel Department and a clerk there looked at my background in psychology, sales, and sales management and said I had some pretty good experience but was not really qualified to work in their factory. I asked about a sales job. They asked if I used their products. I said, "No." "Well," they said, "with that thinking we don't believe you can sell our products. That might be a little problem." The Personnel Clerk had arbitrarily decided I was unqualified to work for their company.

So I went to another large employer headquartered in the city. At the end of the interview, they asked me a similar question. The response and the outcome of the interview was the same.

Finally, I went to work for a small distribution house, selling industrial and commercial kitchen equipment and commercial furnishings. I represented them for a couple of years while I pursued my graduate studies; it kept me close to home and also put me in touch with a lot of different types of businesses. After I had been with this company about six months we were solicited to join the Chamber of Commerce. They were just a small company but they agreed to join, and yours truly was assigned to be the Chamber "point person."

I showed up at my first Chamber meeting and said, "What would you like me to do?" They told me they wanted me to work with the membership committee. What they really wanted me to do was sell Chamber memberships. I said, "Wait a minute. I have one selling job and do *not* need another one." They said, "You don't understand. We're going to give you 15 to 20 leads a month, about half of them in the restaurant business in the area." They had just thrown Brer Rabbit into the proverbial briar patch.

My equipment sales went up immediately, *and* I discovered that I was pretty good at selling Chamber memberships. I also discovered that if you're the leading salesperson of memberships you get invited in once a month to have lunch or breakfast with the board of directors. On our board were the president of a large multi-state bank, the vice chairman of one of the firms to whom I had applied, the executive vice president of the other firm, and many key local executives. Another briar patch of big hitters.

For a couple of months running I was the leading salesperson of Chamber memberships, but then I decided I wanted even *more* visibility, so I did something a little dramatic. I sold more new memberships than all the other 12 people on the committee combined. At the next board meeting I got an extra helping of chicken and beans and was requested to give a little speech about why I had worked so hard for the Chamber and why I was so enthusiastic about it. Here's what the people in the audience saw: a 30-something young man, graduate student at a demanding private school, full-time sales representative, husband and father, reasonably good public speaker, and a person that had worked hard to sell lots of Chamber memberships.

At the end of my talk, a man walked up to me and said he was the executive vice president at the first company to which I had applied. "You're the kind of young man we'd like to have working for us," he said.

I told him that the Personnel Department at his company had told me that I *wasn't* the kind of young man they'd like working for them. He looked back at me and said, "How would you like to have Personnel reporting to you?"

Moral of the story: *get active and be visible* as quickly as you can. While not every exposure within the network is a prospect, you can build a sphere of influence which can be expanded over time. And when you do get the exposure you're seeking, be prepared to position yourself. Be ready when you've created this exposure for yourself—have your personal positioning statement on the tip of your tongue!

Joan Peurifoy, who is very active in service and civic organizations in Dallas, says that even her husband was skeptical when she announced years ago that she wanted to become involved with these type groups. "He said, 'You won't get any business that way'. Actually, I got one of my biggest clients from a civic organization contact."

The added plus, for Joan and others like her: "I learned a lot about my own community. It's a way to give something *back*."

Develop your position within your networks, build your relationships, and fly with the eagles.

Summary — Chapter 7:

• _The five types of self-marketing campaigns are proactive/reactive, networking, captive seminars, invitation seminars, and referrals._

• _Combining proactive (i.e. cold calling) and reactive (i.e. targeted mailings) techniques will result in warmer, and more powerful, marketing approaches._

• _The steps for a proactive-reactive "combination power campaign" are: define the target group, develop the reactive instrument, implement proactively, follow up, reposition for additional business, and get referrals._

• _The "49 Cent-4 hypothetical" campaign can double the impact of using a hypothetical, a powerful tool for illustrating "real" investments to prospects._

• _The marketing-to-newborns campaign positions you to provide a college funding plan and repositions you to provide a retirement funding vehicle._

• _Self-marketing by establishing your own network for interface with people who influence asset holders will put you in touch with those in non-related professions with whom you may end up sharing a client that is valuable to both of you._

• _Self-marketing through a network already in place — cultural organizations, fund raising drives, chambers of commerce, and the like — will give you broad exposure to those who control significant assets._

8

SEMINARS — FROM FRUSTRATION TO FRUITION

In an old city by the storied shores
Where the bright summit of Olympus soars,
A cryptic statue mounted towards the light—
Heel-winged, tip-toed, and poised for instant flight.

"O statue, tell your name," a traveler cried,
And solemnly the marble lips replied:
"Men call me Opportunity: I lift
My winged feet from earth to show how swift
My flight, how short my stay—
How Fate is ever waiting on the way."

"But why that tossing ringlet on your brow?"
"That men may seize me any moment: Now,
NOW is my other name: to-day my date:
O traveler, to-morrow is too late!"

Edwin Markham,
"The Gates of Paradise and Other Poems"

8

"When I first started out, I was absolutely lost. I did $24,000 gross my first year in the business. I was ready to get out, to call it quits. But I finally found something that worked, and still does. It's seminars."

Seminars? "But Les, you pretty much trashed them in the early chapters of this book." No — I criticized bad seminars: poorly thought out ones with no real "targeted" message and the shotgun approach to getting people there. Good ones can work, and very well — as witness the testimony above, which is from Skip Massengill, an extremely successful broker in Philadelphia.

There are are two types of marketing-oriented seminars — **captive** and **by invitation**. But wait, you're asking, aren't all seminars captive? After all, you do have them held in a room with all eyes on you. NO!

A **captive seminar**, as a marketing tool, is a powerful campaign that puts you in front of a group or organization whose charter purpose is other than your seminar. In other words, the Metro Amalgamated Dry Cleaners Association may have been intact and meeting regularly long before you ever decided they needed to hear your message. Generally, the members of organizations before whom you would most want to speak meet regularly for group education, enrichment, and networking, and they are usually appreciative of professional speakers — "outside experts" — who bring information of current appeal to the constituency. As Dr. Thomas Stanley notes, many millionaires are hard-working entrepreneurs at the hands-on controls of their businesses who frequent trade shows or conferences of business owners or other professionals as a means of seeking advice and wisdom about how to improve both their businesses *and* personal lives.

Speaking in front of association- or conference-sponsored groups positions you immediately as an expert *if* you are properly prepared and your presence and message are polished. In the same way that the "messages" in editorial material in a magazine or newspaper are considered to have higher credibility than those in paid advertisements, the position of being a speaker brought in by an organization carries an implicit endorsement. Any presentation to a captive seminar group requires diligent research, well-organized information, and polished speaking skills. (If you haven't done a lot of public speaking, don't assume you can "give it a whirl" in front of business owners or professionals in a captive seminar — go to Toastmasters first.)

Let's assume that in your city there's an association for small business owners in front of whom you'd like to speak. What should your message and your strategy be? Remember, first you have to get them to open up their minds.

The single most important thing in the world to a small business owner, other than his or her family, is REVENUE. It's not taxes; it's not cost control; it's not even profits, because if there isn't any revenue there won't be any taxes or cost control or profits to worry over. Here's a positioning statement that will arouse the curiosity of all closely held business owners: "I design and implement systems that can enhance corporate revenues."

How do you do that? Well, where do revenues come from? "Sales of goods and services." And where do the goods and services that are sold come from? EMPLOYEES. They are the absolutely critical element in the revenue chain in *any* type of business. That's who produces the goods or delivers the services that are sold — which produces revenue. That's who can also "take the revenue away." *Employees produce the revenues of every business in this entire country.* (The employee pension, profit-sharing, and retirement marketplace is only a three trillion dollar one; you might want some of that.)

If you are persistent and fortunate enough to get in front of a small business owner and you try out the above positioning statement on him or her, you are likely to get this response: "How do you do that?"

Before you read this book and got better focused on marketing, as opposed to selling, your response might have been: "I sell 401(k) plans to small business owners."

You would lose this prospect because you would have given a product response — *your* point of view, not his or hers.

By the way, don't tell him you can help keep his employees happy. To put it bluntly, while he doesn't wish them ill, he can't really focus on whether they're happy, and you can't do it anyway. What he really cares about is the productivity of those employees because if they don't produce there's no job for anyone. But you can't really improve their productivity either.

What can you do?

You can help this business owner *retain key employees* by putting together a thorough company pension plan—one that will actually *cost* key employees money if they leave. "I convert today's key employees into long-term employees." That positioning statement speaks to revenue, and gives you the long-term perspective he is looking for — he needs committed employees on his team. You have just unlocked the door to his curious and revenue-driven mind.

If you want to do captive seminars and you target small business owners, focus on employees and revenue. The content of your captive seminar to small business owners focused on employees and revenues *might* consist of the following general areas:

- Money and its uses.
- How inflation impacts the particular type of business.
- Interest rates and their effects on this type of business.
- Import/Export strategies for growth of the business.

It is absolutely imperative that you do your research and your homework so that you can develop a presentation or series of presentations which demonstrate that you have a grasp of the issues facing certain industries or businesses and that show *how* you can help impact revenue in a positive way. Polish your presentation style so that you close with impact, and then follow up, follow up, follow up. (Do not try to sell any products!) You'll get invited back.

Many people, and correctly so, advise that you write articles or columns for trade publications—particularly those of most interest to small business owners. If you are able to do so, be sure you then mail copies of your articles to business owner prospects, which will set the stage for follow-up conversations.

Invitation seminars, in contrast to captive seminars, are those *you* "design" — both the presentation and the audience. Let me say right up front that a "by invitation" seminar is a frequently mis-

understood and misused vehicle. Some professionals swear by invitation seminars; others swear at
the thought of having to put one on.
    Invitation seminars are *not* "group selling."
Rather, a more appropriate description of an invitation seminar might be group "education, information distribution, and credibility building." The
power of an invitation seminar is that it allows
you to "profile" yourself to a small homogeneous
group of people and to present a focused message
that has appeal to these attendees. Rather than the
"all things to all people" approach, an invitation
seminar is more the "one thing to one small group
of people" approach. The greatest appeal of this
type seminar is its multiplier effect — that of geo-
metrically multiplying the one-on-one exposure of
you, the professional.
    The multiplier effect has certainly worked its
power and magic on Skip Massengill over the years.
    Like many new financial service professionals,
Skip first tried classic cold calling as a means of
marketing, but it just didn't work for him. And,
after all, he notes, "consumers themselves can pick
up the phone, dial a toll-free number, and get pretty
much whatever information about a product they
want, at their convenience and 'on their own
terms'." So Skip turned to seminars. "I decided I
liked the exposure. I still do. Seminars are much
more about marketing, and this is a marketing game,
not a selling game. There's a huge difference in the
two."

Skip's definition of selling versus marketing is in line with what we've learned about the more upscale consumer and *why* he or she buys.

"Selling is when you actively, aggressively promote or distribute information based on the seller's objective rather than the buyer's objective," he says. "Marketing is the matching of products, or tools, with financial objectives, desires, and needs of the client. It's an education process, and it's ongoing."

Indeed, most financial service professionals who are successful with seminars approach them from the standpoint of education for clients and prospects, not places to tout plans or products.

Bill Kissinger, of Kissinger Financial, has also had great success with seminars. His "angle" is doing them in cooperation with and under the auspices of a local community college, which further reinforces the education message. At a recent Kissinger Financial seminar, 23 people attended — 22 made appointments.

"Tell me very many other ways by which you could get 22 new clients in a month, real live individuals who walk through the door with a net worth of a million dollars?", asks Bill.

In Skip Massengill's case, he began by targeting specific consumers in specific geographic areas in his metropolitan area. "We figured the high net worth person was probably already dealing with a First Boston-type company, so we tried to get the people that were being 'missed' — a person that had a couple of large Certificates of Deposit, didn't have a broker or advisor, and just didn't know what to do."

After several years of trial and error, Skip and his associates have developed several large mailing lists: eight zones of 10,000 names each. "We pinpoint the zone each time, take a look at the demographics, and discuss what we need to talk about with that particular group." The seminar promotion gets a valuable boost from Skip's show each morning on a local Philadelphia radio station.

Skip does the majority of his seminars in the spring and fall, two to three every month. They're free for attendees, who usually number about 100 people each seminar. Skip's average "closing ratio" for his seminars? "Out of 100 people, there are probably 60 buying units — 20 are 'lost', 20 don't have any money, 20 become clients over the next six months to a year. If you educate them, show them ways to help themselves, and present concepts only, you'll get them there — and you'll turn them into clients."

Skip unquestionably has his seminar process down to a fine art, which further illustrates that to do seminars right you have to target, target, target, and refine, refine, refine.

"Professionals who have no luck with seminars are those just sending out 2,000 mailers to people at random and hoping they show up," Skip says. "If you send out 2,000 mailers with little thought about to whom they're going, you'd better be prepared to have an empty room."

Despite Skip's and Bill's and many others' success with seminars, they are not for everybody. Jay Batcha of First of Michigan, also a very successful broker, says he has had "varying success" with seminars. "My feeling is that you have to do them all the time to do them well. If you do two a year you may be reinventing the wheel each time and you can never 'pay yourself' for the hours you put in."

Seminars are hard work and they take a lot of planning. If you're considering some seminar marketing, first, recognize that you *won't* be an overnight success. It took Skip many years to perfect his style and his approach. Here are some basic rules of thumb to consider as you plan for doing seminars.

The **first rule of thumb** in planning to do seminar marketing is to target a group by profile; they must be *as alike as possible.* If you want "little old blue-haired ladies," do not try to mix them in with "divorced professionals." Get all little old blue-haired ladies, and remember that a group of 25-30 is best for eye contact. With target marketing you want small groups and you want *all of them and all of their business.*

Second rule of thumb for seminars: always have a client there. It adds to your credibility and it never hurts to have an "amen corner!"

Third rule of thumb: if at all possible, send handwritten invitations instead of self-stick labels on company envelopes run through the postage meter. (That will also keep you from the temptation of sending out too many!) Then follow up: call, call, call. You should place your first call three days after you've mailed the invitations, the second two days prior to the seminar, and the third the morning of the seminar (or the evening before if your seminar is in the morning).

Fourth rule of thumb (especially if you're not Skip Massengill or Bill Kissinger — yet!): have someone "special" — not you — make the presentation. Your concepts should be presented by another expert: an insurance agent, a product wholesaler, a CPA. *Your task is to sell this group on coming to see and learn from this expert.* The expert's task is to educate them on concepts and to convey to them in a non-selling manner (no products!) what has to happen to fill their needs.

Your expert can say, "If you want specific information on how to implement this, you can talk to my friend Mike, who has been kind enough to host this group." Your expert is "back-selling" you. "Mike implements campaigns just like these for people like you. He has over 20 years experience in this business. I'm sure he'll be glad to take a few minutes to chat with you when we're done and to make an appointment to see you." Your expert can sell you *better* in a group setting like a seminar.

Final rule of thumb for an invitation seminar: be available and be ready. *Be ready to write business.* I'm amazed at how many financial service professionals I've worked with who say they've never done any business on the spot. Let me tell you a story about how that can backfire on you.

When I first came on board with my company, one of my first trips was to California with one of our wholesalers. We had been invited to make a presentation to a seminar hosted by a local broker. Our attendees were older people in a rather exclusive retirement community — 65 people in all — and the theme was maximizing retirement income. The community association provided the meeting place and even paid for the wine, cheese, and melon balls. The broker had virtually no cost in this seminar. Not a bad deal and a group we'd all like to be in front of.

After the presentations, the host broker thanked everyone for coming and said she'd be in touch next week. As we were standing around having refreshments, this little old man came up to her, reached in his pocket, pulled out a money market checkbook, and said, "That fund you were talking about looks awfully good. I think I'd like to have some of that. It looks like I could adjust my income from 6 to 8 to 10 percent as my needs would require."

The broker said, "That's true." He then said he'd like to have some of it. She said, "I'll call you next week."

To an old hard-nosed salesman like me this was almost enough to induce a heart attack. This is not rocket science. *TAKE THE CHECK!*

We got back to San Francisco several days later and reviewed the sales reports from the prior few days. Seems this little old man found an available and willing broker. He walked into the local office of a major brokerage firm, found the broker of the day, showed him the prospectus on our fund which he had received at the presentation, and said, "I'd like some of this."

Guess what the broker did? *HE TOOK THE CHECK*. It was for $287,000 — and a gross commission of approximately $10,000 to that broker who had never seen this prospect before.

We clipped and forwarded a copy of the trade to the broker who had not been ready to take the check.

No one will ever again have to tell her to be ready to do business.

Take new account cards, take applications, take pens, take disclosure forms. Be ready to take the check. Somebody, at some seminar, at some time in the future, will try to give you one. Isn't that what you want?

Summary — Chapter 8:

• *A captive seminar is a power campaign that gives you quality exposure to a group or organization that was in place before you came along.*

• *Speaking in front of a professional organization, conference, or trade group carries an implicit third-party endorsement.*

• *Invitation seminars are those you design — both the presentation and the audience. They are based on group education, information distribution, and credibility building.*

• *There are several common sense rules of thumb for seminars:*

  - *One, target a small group of people whose "profile" is that they are as alike as possible.*
  - *Two, always have a client present.*
  - *Three, send personalized invitations.*
  - *Four, have an outside expert make the presentation on concepts only — no products!*
  - *Five, be ready to take a check!*

9

IF YOU BUILD IT
THEY WILL COME

"We are advertis'd by our loving friends."

William Shakespeare

9

How many times in your career in financial services have you been told to "get a referral"? It may sound old hat, but referrals are a campaign in and of themselves, at the top of the marketing campaign pyramid. Referrals as a means of self-marketing are those that have the most appeal to the upscale consumer because they are predicated on a long-term trust relationship. They are powerful and can drive your business to new heights.

Ask successful financial service professionals about how they achieved their success and you will likely hear referrals as one major contributing factor. Jay Batcha believes firmly that "if a client is happy, they'll send you other people. It will come to you."

Joan Peurifoy has had good success with referrals from other professionals, but reminds that it's a two-way street : "We shouldn't always approach it from the standpoint of being on the receiving end."

Brian Lee discovered several years ago that focusing on referrals would greatly increase his client base and revenue. "I didn't have to be a rocket scientist to realize that if I put more emphasis on referral business my revenue would go up." Brian, the golfer, says that golfing and referrals have turned out to be his biggest source of business.

"I've gotten a lot of big clients from '$100 referrals'. If a client tells me I ought to go see so-and-so, I do, but I let that person know I'm there out of courtesy to their friend. It positions me as a professional who is really taking care of my client — *their friend*. Some new clients that I have actually represent the '12th generation' of referrals — families, friends, business colleagues. I never push hard but I also tell people that if I climb across the table and jump in their face there's a reason — at least listen to me. I've got a 95 to 98 percent success ratio once I get in front of someone to whom I've been referred."

Even Skip Massengill, the Philadelphia seminar king, relies on referrals. "Everybody that you know and with whom you have a relationship has some money and some needs. People talk, on a conceptual basis, with their peers about what they're doing. The only hard part about referrals is that all consumers want to believe they're *already* dealing with the best." Perception vs reality, again!

Jerome Schneider, president of American National Securities, Inc. of Beverly Hills, Calif., says that there are numerous techniques for generating referrals from existing clients, and, writing in Investment Advisor magazine, offers these suggestions:

• Make referrals a part of the payment for your services, advising clients up front that you expect, say, three referrals if you do a good job.

• Ask clients if they'd be willing to sponsor an afternoon tea, a morning coffee, or a cocktail hour for their friends, during which you could talk about a particular concept or service.

• Any time a client makes a decision to move into a particular investment, ask if he or she knows of anyone else who might benefit from such an opportunity.

• Any time you mail promotional or informational materials to existing clients, enclose an extra copy and ask them to pass it on to an interested friend or associate.

• Ask your client to bring a friend and join you for a sporting event, a play, or some other entertainment.

• Ask satisfied clients to write a letter of referral for you — and provide copies of several sample letters they can use to ensure they make the points you want covered.

Was It Good For You?

Obviously, the object of the referral game is to get as many as possible, and when you've been told, in many cases by a manager, to "get a referral", you've probably been told to get 6, 10, 20.

I certainly don't disagree with that, but I am telling you that you really need to get *only two* and you should get them from the upper half of your client account book of 200. You don't need the "little" ones from the bottom half; you've already got too many of those. The reason you want them from the people at the top is that you want *people just like them.*

The two referrals I suggest you go after are one *internal* and one *external*. When I talk with financial service professionals about internal referrals, most people assume "family." No; it's closer in than even that — it's *the client*. I want you to say to this client, "Listen, the last time we did business together, it was good for both of us. *When can we do it again?*"

Don't forget that you are also in the retention business. A recent survey done by the Securities Industry Association found that 89 percent of the time clients do not leave brokers, planners, or agents that have assisted them with at least three different types of investments. Not three stocks or three mutual funds — three different types. "*When can we do it again?*"

Every client you have at the top of your book has more money and on-going needs and financial goals. I submit to you that if you don't know right now when you're going to do *more* business with the top 10 percent of your clients you are not in the service business, you are in the order-taking business.

Will It Be Good For Your Friends?

How you ask for additional business from your current clients — *external* referrals — is critical. Most financial service professionals tend to think of asking for referrals strictly from their point of view — you know: "Would you help me build my book of clients? Gosh, I could really use some help." Frankly, your clients don't really give a darn about you and your book of business, but they do give a darn about themselves and their close friends. You must change your thinking from *them* helping *you*. Instead, you must position you and your expertise as a way to help their friends and business associates find the same solutions you have provided to them: "Perhaps you have friends or business associates who are not getting the kinds of returns they'd like on the investments they have in place. You could use my expertise as a way to help your friends receive the kind of returns they ought to be getting. Can you think of someone that you think I should be helping?"

In asking for an external referral, a name and phone number is not enough. You want a face to face introduction, to be personally introduced by the top asset holders in your client roster to one other person they know well. Experience tells us that upwards of 80 percent of the time when you get a face to face introduction that person will do business with you. (Only 20 to 30 percent of telephone or mail referrals will.)

Let's assume client Barbara has just mentioned her old college roommate, Joan. Suggest that the three of you have breakfast next week. Why breakfast? Because everybody is fresh, you can feed three people for $25, and nobody has too much to drink. In addition, you can follow up in the afternoon without seeming too pushy, using language like this:

"It was certainly a pleasure to meet you this morning. Barbara has been a client and friend of mine for a number of years and it was great meeting one of her close friends. If I come across investment ideas that look like they might be appealing to you, would you like to hear about them?"

What is Joan going to say? "Yes, of course I would." You now have your opening to market yourself. You have been given permission *by the prospect* to market to her, and you have just received a *transfer of trust* from your client, the referral's friend.

It takes a considerable amount of time and effort to build up trust with a "cold" prospect, but a transfer of trust from a referral is quick and powerful. In the same way that you have an instantaneous "connection" with a friend of a friend, you will also have a connection, a bond, with a referral from a current client. With an external referral, your most powerful clients are providing you with a third-party endorsement, helping you do your qualifying and further building your personal profile.

After you get the desired personal introduction from your good client Barbara, you owe her something — a big thank you. If she has provided you with a face to face introduction over a meal, your thank you should be formal and generous — flowers, an excellent bottle of wine, tickets to a sporting event or concert, and a very sincere handwritten note. This is not only good business manners, it is reinforcement of positive behavior. What's the likelihood a person will repeat a behavior that is positively reinforced? Everyone likes to be thanked — do it.

If you have relationships with your top clients that are based on trust, referrals will transfer that trust to a new prospect. Referrals are the top of the marketing campaign pyramid. They can put *you* on top.

Summary — Chapter 9:

• _Referrals as a type of self-marketing are those that have the most appeal to the upscale consumer because they are predicated on a long-term trust relationship._

• _There are really only two types of referrals you should try for: internal (the client) and external (the client's friends, family, business colleagues)._

• _A recent Securities Industry Association found that 89 percent of the time clients do not leave brokers, planners, or agents that have assisted them with at least three different types of investments._ _"When can we do it again?"_

• _How you ask for a referral from a current valuable client is critical — your clients aren't really concerned with helping you build your book of business._

• _A referral from a valued client provides a transfer of trust._

10

HALF FULL OR
HALF EMPTY?

*"Hold to the course, though the storms are
about you;
Stick to the road where the banner still flies;
Fate and his legions are ready to rout you —
Give 'em both barrels — and aim for their eyes.*

*Life's not a rose bed, a dream, or a bubble,
A living in clover beneath cloudless skies;
And Fate hates a fighter who's looking for trouble,
So give 'im both barrels — and shoot for the eyes.*

*Fame never comes to the loafers and sitters,
Life's full of knots in a shifting disguise;
Fate only picks on the cowards and quitters,
So give 'em both barrels — and aim for the eyes."*

Grantland Rice

10

To paraphrase Charles Dickens, it is both the best of times and the worst of times.

On the one hand . . . .

"I think this business will get easier. Consumers are learning more about what we provide and the more educated the public gets the better off we'll be. In the future, we'll have to do less convincing of people that they need our services. Twenty years from now, it will be 'of course I need your counsel'." — Jim Wisner, Financial Service Corporation

"In many ways, this is an ideal time to start in this business. There are zillions of dollars out there looking for a good place to go and a good person to guide it. People are smarter, and they want specialists, professionals with whom they can have a long-term relationship." — Jay Batcha, First of Michigan

"You've got to believe in magic. You've got to help your clients believe in magic. Make no mistake, clients are going to get a lot smarter, but that process will make professionals in the industry much better. It's a wonderful time to be in business." — Bill Kissinger, Kissinger Financial

"The best thing that has happened in our industry is that everyone — clients and advisors — has learned trees don't always grow to the sky. Expectations are getting better, more realistic." — Jay Lewis, Nathan & Lewis

On the other hand . . . .

"Banks are in the driver's seat. The common accumulation products clients want they can all get at a bank right now. And banks are in a position of trust; people believe in them." — Jim Wisner, Financial Service Corporation

"Competition is getting more fierce. Consumers have much more knowledge of no-load funds and they want them. The perception is that they're 'free'. It's like saying: 'let's get a plumber to fix the roof — and see if he'll do it for nothing'." — Skip Massengill, Butcher & Singer

"I believe that, unfortunately, a lot of new brokers and financial planners will have to sell four or five times as much in the future to get the same revenue as they do now." — Jay Batcha, First of Michigan

And then there are all those gloom and doom stories in the business and consumer press. To wit: "The Broken Promise of Financial Planning," (Money magazine, November 1992)   sternly advises that " . . . there is still a disturbing shortage of advisers

Americans can turn to with confidence. Sadly, all too many clients have found that the promise of financial planning — that you can hand over your finances to a caring professional who will put your interests first — is made to be broken. Citing statistics, regulators estimate that planners cause clients to lose at least $600 million every two years." (And, as Joan Peurifoy notes, "make no mistake: your clients *do* read Money magazine.")

An article in Financial Services Week (October 5, 1992), "Poll: 30% of Americans Eschew Use of Financial Professionals," contains more disturbing news. A survey conducted by the Institute of Certified Financial Planners (ICFP) found that, of consumers interviewed, "financial professionals" rated highest were bankers (14%), financial planners (12%), accountants (10%), brokers (9%), attorneys (7%), and insurance agents (4%). Fourteen percent of the people surveyed said they wouldn't go to *anyone.*

Is this a half-full or a half-empty glass? I submit to you that it is half-full — and *you can fill it to the top.* Challenges always mean opportunities.

To fill this half-full glass, you must market yourself as the *only viable alternative to filling the needs of your prospects and clients* and you must have a well-orchestrated plan, using some or all of the strategies I've tried to present in this book. It won't happen overnight and nobody — least of all me — is saying it's easy. Marketing yourself requires long-term vision, commitment, dedication, and patience. There is no "One Minute Marketer." This notion of vision — the vision you must have of *you as the product* your clients and prospects want — reminds me of a story. (One last one, please!) A young boy watched intently day after day, fascinated, as the artist Michelangelo sculpted his beautiful David. When the finished piece finally "emerged", the young boy said to Michelangelo, "But how did you know he was in there?"

Bill Kissinger, president of Kissinger Financial Services, like other successful veterans of our business, has learned some marketing truths, some lessons about vision, the hard way.

"Prior to the 'crash' of 1987, we just got tons of referrals," Bill says. "But all of a sudden, it dried to a trickle. I was dumbfounded. And then it dawned on me that we did not really have a marketing plan other than just passing out business cards, doing some luncheons, and receiving referrals. Now, we have one staff person who does nothing but *work on the future* — doing marketing all the time."

In his book "Guerrilla Marketing: Secrets For Making Big Profits From Your Small Business," author Jay Conrad Levinson offers some excellent thoughts on embarking on and committing to a long-term marketing plan:

"Ten Truths You Must Never Forget"

(1) *The market is constantly changing.* New families, new prospects, new lifestyles change the

marketplace. Nearly one-third of the people in America will move this year. Nearly five million Americans will get married. When you stop advertising, you miss evolving opportunities and stop being part of the process. You are not on the bus. You are not in the game.

(2) *People forget fast.* Remember, they're bombarded with tons of messages (an estimated 2700) daily. An experiment proved the need for constancy in marketing by running advertising once a week for 13 weeks. After that period, 63 percent of the people surveyed remembered the advertising. One month later, 32 percent recalled it. Two weeks after that, 21 percent remembered it. That means 79 percent forgot it.

(3) *Your competition isn't quitting.* People will spend money to make purchases, and if you don't make them aware that you are selling something, they'll spend their money elsewhere.

(4) *Marketing strengthens your identity.* When you quit marketing, you shortchange your reputation, reliability, and the confidence people have in you. When economic conditions turn sour, smart companies continue to advertise. The bond of communication is too precious to break capriciously.

(5) *Marketing is essential to survival and growth.* With very few exceptions, people won't know you're there if you don't get the word out. And when you cease marketing, you're on the path to nonexistence. Just as you can't start a business

without marketing, you can't maintain one without it.

(6) *Marketing enables you to hold on to your old customers.* Many enterprises survive on repeat and referral business. Old customers are the key to both. When old customers don't hear *from* you or *about* you, they tend to forget you.

(7) *Marketing maintains morale.* Your own morale is improved when you see your marketing at work, and especially when you see that it does, indeed, work. Your employees' morale is similarly uplifted. And cutting out marketing seems a signal of failure to those who actively follow your advertising. That won't be many people, but it will be some.

(8) *Marketing gives you an advantage over competitors who have ceased marketing.* A troubled economy can be a superb advantage to a marketing-minded entrepreneur. It forces some competitors to stop marketing — giving you a chance to pull ahead of them and attract some of their customers. In all ugly economic situations, there are winners and losers.

(9) *Marketing allows your business to continue operating.* You still have overhead: telephone bills, yellow pages ads, rent and/or equipment costs, possibly a payroll, your time. Marketing creates the air overhead breathes.

(10) *You have invested money that you stand to lose.* If you quit marketing, all of the money you spent for ads, commercials, and advertising time

and space becomes lost as the consumer aware-ness it purchased slowly dwindles away. Sure, you can buy it again. But you'll have to start from scratch. Unless you are planning to go out of business, it is rarely a good idea to cease marketing completely. (From "Guerrilla Marketing," by Jay Conrad Levinson, © 1984 by Jay Conrad Levinson. Reprinted by permission of Houghton Mifflin Company. All rights reserved.)

If you embrace your marketing plan as a *long-term, growth-oriented investment in yourself* (much the same way you want your clients to) you will see the payoff down the road. After all, people don't run out of financial services like they do toothpaste or soap. Be there when *they're* ready to switch.

You will be, if you commit some time—10 percent of every day—to your marketing game plan. To help you *get* started and *stay* focused, here are some simple marketing implementation worksheets. Keep them handy, and *use* them.

Chapter 10

Self-Marketing Action Plan

• *Identify* several target markets. Those target markets should, where possible, relate to your "personal success profile."

• *Build a profile* of each of those target markets.

• *Develop positioning statements* which will address the target market profile.

• *Decide on what approach method* is appropriate and how that method should be implemented.

TARGET MARKETS DEFINED
(Should Not Exceed 200 people) :
A) Demographic characteristics: _____

_____

_____

_____

_____

B) Geographic characteristics: _____

_____

_____

_____

_____

What do you know about this market or the people in this market? What are their financial goals, common lifestyle characteristics, and/or consumer buying habits? Describe these people in as much detail as possible._____

_____

_____

_____

_____

_____

TARGET MARKETS DEFINED

FOLLOW-UP PROFILE, IDENTIFY NEEDS—e.g. What do they want to have happen?

TARGET MARKET #1

A) What type of business or industry are they in? How does the business operate? How do external economic factors affect it?

_____

_____

_____

_____

_____

_____

B) What are their personal financial needs?

_____

_____

_____

_____

_____

C) What secondary need exists or will arise later?

_____

_____

_____

_____

TARGET MARKETS
POSITIONING STATEMENTS

Target Market #1
a)Personal: _____

_____

b) Company: _____

_____

c) Product: _____

_____

Target Market #2
a)Personal: _____

_____

b) Company: _____

_____

c) Product: _____

_____

Target Market #3
a)Personal: _____

_____

b) Company: _____

_____

c) Product: _____

_____

TARGET MARKETS
METHOD OF "APPROACH"

For each target market, jot down some ideas on
how you might implement each of the five types of
self-marketing campaigns:

Target Market # 1
a) Proactive/Reactive _____

_____

_____

b) Networking _____

_____

_____

c) Captive Seminars _____

_____

_____

d) Invitation Seminars _____

_____

_____

e) Referrals _____

_____

_____

TARGET MARKETS
METHOD OF "APPROACH"

Target Market # 2

a) Proactive/Reactive _____

_____

_____

_____

b) Networking _____

_____

_____

_____

c) Captive Seminars _____

_____

_____

_____

d) Invitation Seminars _____

_____

_____

_____

e) Referrals _____

_____

_____

_____

TARGET MARKETS
CHECK SYSTEM

Once your profiles, positioning statements, and action techniques are decided, set up a check system:

• Have a peer review your self-marketing plan and make comments: _____

_____

_____

_____

_____

_____

• Have a manager review your self-marketing plan and make comments: _____

_____

_____

_____

_____

_____

• Have a product sponsor review your self-marketing plan and make comments: _____

_____

_____

_____

_____

_____

NOTES

The Sandwich Generation Beckons

The opportunities for marketing yourself, for filling that glass to the top, are virtually limitless. As the number of professionals in the industry with the long-term vision, stamina, and dedication is contracting, the marketplace — consumers with financial goals and needs and who need a relationship with a trusted advisor — is actually expanding. The aging baby boomer population, whose leading edge is poised to hit 50 in 1996, is a massive group — 82 million people — with unique expectations, lifestyles, and financial needs. Facing the middle to late stages of both middle age and careers, the need for immediate financial planning and asset accumulation will be acute. Middle age (usually defined as beginning about age 45) is usually the time when individuals begin to think about asset protection and retirement savings. This generation also faces two additional threshholds, both with significant consequences for financial services professionals.

First, this "sandwich generation" is increasingly being squeezed by time and financial pressures from their children on one end and their parents on the other. Second, the baby boom generation as a whole stands to receive a huge transfer of wealth from their parents. Economists conservatively predict that as much as $8 trillion in assets could be transferred from aging or deceased parents to the next generation over the next 20 years. Currently, nearly 70 percent of all wealth is in the hands of people over 50 years old and the *median* net worth of those 55 to 64 is $90,000 today. It's no wonder people are calling the baby boomers "the new inheritors." Who will manage all the money? Who will help them with their own assets accumulating in 40l(k) or 403(b) plans? *Who will get all these new clients?*

If this glass doesn't look half full to you . . . . it does to your competition.

How you market yourself successfully depends to a large extent on your own personality, your own strengths and weaknesses, your target markets, your experience, and your BAVI, but it also depends on how well you apply the concepts and principles that have been discussed in this book. It is my sincere hope that you have learned some new approaches to thinking about marketing and the marketplace that will help take your business to new levels. It is also my sincere hope that you won't disregard the many fine skills you are already using effectively. There is simply no substitute for the tried and true. Or, as Brian Lee so aptly puts it: "The current buzzword in the industry is 'relationship selling'. Well, I've been sitting around kitchen tables for 10 years. If that's relationship selling, I'll keep on doing it."

Amen.

INDEX

Interviews with Practicing Professionals:

REFERENCED BOOKS

Girard, Joe, "How To Sell Yourself," Simon & Schuster, Inc., p. 47

Le Boeuf, Michael, Ph.D., "How To Win Customers and Keep Them For Life," Berkley Books, p. 54-55

Levinson, Jay Conrad, "Guerrilla Marketing," Houghton Mifflin Company, p. 202-205

Levitt, Theodore, "The Marketing Imagination," The Free Press, p. 44

Ries, Al and Trout, Jack, "Positioning: The Battle For Your Mind," "Marketing Warfare," and "Bottom Up Marketing," McGraw-Hill, Inc., p. 49, 50, 62-63, 136-137

Stanley, Thomas J., Ph.D., "Marketing To The Affluent," Dow Jones-Irwin, p. 98-101

Von Clausewitz, Carl, "On War," Penguin Books, Ltd., p. 62

Wollack, Richard and Parisse, Alan, "Power Marketing," Dearborn Financial Publishing, Inc., p. 130-132

Zuker, Elaina, "The Seven Secrets of Influence," McGraw-Hill, Inc., p. 138-144